The Book on Writing

The Ultimate Guide to Writing Well

ALSO BY PAULA LaROCQUE

Chalk Line, a Ben Gallagher Mystery

On Words: Insight Into How Our Words Work—and Don't

Championship Writing: 50 Ways to Improve Your Writing

The Book on Writing

The Ultimate Guide to Writing Well

Paula LaRocque

GREY & GUVNOR PRESS

Library of Congress Cataloging-in-Publication Data
LaRocque, Paula
The book on writing: the ultimate guide to writing well / by Paula LaRocque
p. cm.
Includes index.
ISBN 978-0-9892367-0-6
1. Authorship. I. Title.
PN4775.L288 2003
808.02--dc21
2003013308

Printed in the United States of America

Author photo © 2010 Kevin Bearden
Cover design: Anne Locascio
ISBN: 0989236706
ISBN 13: 978-0-9892367-0-6
ISBN (ebook) 978-0-9892367-1-3

Grey and Guvnor Press
Arlington, Texas

www.paulalarocque.com

Praise for *The Book on Writing*

"LaRocque's advice is sane and sound. . . . Beginning writers should find clear, useful advice here."

—Publishers Weekly

"A clear and concise guide." *(Kindle Edition)*

—Library Journal

"Paula LaRocque offers her impressive expertise in *The Book On Writing: The Ultimate Guide To Writing Well* . . . an excellent and highly recommended guide to clarity of thought and printed word."

—Midwest Book Review

"Paula LaRocque understands the way to elegant, artful storytelling is simple, basic, accurate words used sparingly and with purpose. She demonstrates why clarity, simplicity, and dignity top flabby construction and corpulent descriptives every time. *The Book on Writing* is THE book on writing."

—Bob Giles, curator, Nieman Foundation for Journalism
Harvard University

"This book is well-organized, cleanly written, and keenly insightful. It embraces the whole of writing—whether of great novelists or office managers . . . This is really good and useful stuff."

—Allen Pusey, editor and publisher
ABA Journal, American Bar Association

"Don't waste your time arguing with Paula LaRocque's advice. Just read, learn, and do. It's a guarantee you WILL write well and your readers will get well in the process."

—Tom Sylvestri, president
Community Newspapers, Media General, Inc.

[*The Book on Writing* was chosen by the American Booksellers Association for its Top Ten list as well as for the highly influential "Book Sense 76" list. The Writer's Web Watch also named *The Book on Writing* No. 1 of the top six books published in 2003.]

This book is for my son, David
For my sisters Keeta and Mona
And in memory of Andrea, my little girl lost

Contents

Section One: Writing Mechanics
A Dozen Guidelines to Good Writing

Section Two: Storytelling Devices

Section Three: A Handbook

The Book on Writing
Author's Note

The Book on Writing: The Ultimate Guide to Writing Well contains the bulk of what I've learned and taught in three decades of working with writers. It is meant to be one-stop shopping for writers working in any genre.

The book consists of three sections, the first of which presents specific principles that I became acquainted with early in my university teaching career and have depended upon since. Those guidelines became clear to me one by one, as I read and corrected thousands of college essays and saw the work break down and become unreadable for this reason or that. The guidelines, which are chiefly mechanical and structural, help bring accuracy, precision, clarity, brevity, warmth, and interest to any writing.

Each chapter of Section One begins with a short and simply stated guideline, followed by discussion and examples from various fields showing how the guideline works in the real world.

Section Two deals with the creative elements of storytelling: narrative writing, story archetype, and literary device; building interest and suspense; description; figurative language and imagery; words and sound; and pace. I've paid particular attention to the role of archetype and literary device in storytelling—including in informational media. Story form in myth and archetype is an exciting, meaningful, and fertile field of study for all writers, but it is sadly neglected and misunderstood.

Section Three presents a clear, concise, and brief handbook that focuses on common problems in grammar, usage, punctuation, and style—problems that often bother even wordsmiths. The handbook is not a comprehensive guide to grammar, style, and usage, but it comprises the material that most often goes awry in writing of all kinds. Section 3's final chapter, "Style Guide," contains answers to the questions I'm most often asked in writing workshops.

I sincerely hope you will find *The Book on Writing* helpful in all your writing—memo, report, feature, or story. My desire throughout was to offer you something that would not only help you achieve accurate, clear, and brief informational writing, but that would also assist you in your creative work, whether fact or fiction.

The flawed examples in this book are real passages, gleaned from publications, reports, and correspondence of all kinds. I've changed the names of people or place or both to protect the identity of writer and publication. Some portions of the book may have previously appeared in a different form in my "Mastering the Art" column for the Society of Professional Journalists' magazine, *Quill*, or in my "Words Matter" column for *The Dallas Morning News*.

I extend my heartfelt gratitude to my husband, Paul, who reads and edits my work with tireless intelligence, generosity, and good cheer. I also thank Emily Boehm, a young woman whom I haven't met but who named this book. She was at the time a student at Kalamazoo College and an intern at Marion Street Press, Inc., and she interviewed me for an article she was writing. During the interview, I mentioned the challenge of finding the right title for my new book. *Any ideas, Emily?* I asked.

"Why don't you call it what you're calling it," she suggested.

"Am I calling it something?"

"You're calling it *The Book on Writing*," she said.

And so I was.

Paula LaRocque
Arlington, Texas
April 2003

WRITING MECHANICS

A Dozen Guidelines to Good Writing

Introduction to the Guidelines

I see but one rule: to be clear. If I am not clear, all my world crumbles to nothing.

—Stendhal, writing to Balzac

I created the writing guidelines in this section of *The Book on Writing* during many years of working with writers and non-writers and discovering what happened when their written communications went wrong. The guidelines are just that—they are not *rules*. Skilled writers know how, when, and why to ignore them, but even the skilled do so only selectively and with particular purpose. Rare exceptions aside, these guidelines will help make your writing clear, brief, precise, purposeful, warm, and interesting. And, because the principles are easy to understand and apply, they're especially useful not only in the editing process but also when you're writing in a hurry.

One critical guideline—that of the need for Standard English—isn't in this section but rather in Section Three. By Standard English, I mean the accepted standards of grammar, punctuation, structure, and usage essential for polished informational or workplace communications. The "code" of Standard English is often violated for special effects in fiction or other creative writing, of course, but we're ill advised to violate it in informational writing of all kinds, including memos, letters, reports, press releases and, usually, ad copy. In any case, the subject of mechanical accuracy is the business of the third part of this book.

Accuracy aside, simplicity, clarity, and brevity are the most important criteria for all writing. Interestingly, few writers balk at the demand for accuracy, but some offer a curious resistance to the demand for simplicity, clarity, and brevity. A CEO given to dense, pretentious, and undisciplined writing once said that following these guidelines would damage his "style." Perhaps unreadable writing could be called a "style," but it's not a style worth cultivating. Fact is, simplicity, clarity, and brevity form the bedrock of *all* good communication, and have for time immemorial. (Never *mind* James Joyce or William Faulkner or even Henry James. I love their work, too—in its place. And its place is not in a memo.)

The two sentences below demonstrate the overall difference between the fuzzy, abstract writing that we see too often in workplace communication, and the simple, clear writing that serves both writer and reader. The first is the writer's original version, and the second is his revision, using the guidelines:

Original: *Prompted in part by a new anti-smog law that is boosting business' demand for better service, a major reassessment that could lead to big changes in the county's public transportation system is beginning.*

Rewritten, following the guidelines: *Local leaders want to make it easier for county residents to get around without their cars.*

Those passages capture in a nutshell the goals of the following guidelines. Those goals are not to "dumb down" our writing; they are to make it immediately clear, meaningful, conversational, and inviting.

CHAPTER 1

A Dozen Guidelines to Good Writing

Keep Sentences Short, Varied, and to One Main Idea

It is easier to be long than short.

—Samuel Butler

Keep sentences short. The period is one of the reader's (and writer's) best friends. In most cases, when a sentence grows to 20 words or so, the writer should start seeking a way to end it. Sentence length *average* is more important than the length of any one sentence, however. Vary sentence length to avoid tedium, but a safe average is probably around 20 words. That means you'll have short sentences (as short as one word), medium-length sentences (12 to 18 words), and longish sentences (18 to 25 words).

But word count doesn't tell the whole story. Look again at the last sentence of the preceding paragraph: *That means you'll have short sentences (as short as one word), medium-length sentences (12 to 18 words), and longish sentences (18 to 25 words).* That sentence has 21 words (not counting numbers), but it qualifies as a "difficult" sentence because of its numbers and its parenthetical interruptions. Those elements disturb natural sentence flow and therefore have a lengthening, even muddying, effect. Does this mean that I need short, crisp sentences before and after that 21-word sentence? Yes.

Notice the ploy I just used. Instead of making a statement, I asked a question—*Does this mean I need short sentences before and after that 21-word sentence?* Not only was that question short and simple, but it allowed me to answer with a one-word sentence: *Yes.* That kind of pacing gives the reader a rest. It also is more interesting because it adds variety—the kind of variety natural in speech.

The above three paragraphs have an average sentence length of 13.5, a reading grade level of 7.7, and a Flesch Reading Ease score of 63.3. (Studies show that most Americans—even the highly educated—prefer to read at a grade level of 10 or below, and that a suitable score on the Flesch readability index is between 60 and 70.) So all things being equal—that is, if the subject is unforbidding and the vocabulary familiar—what I've written so far should be clear at first reading.

Am I suggesting that you consider every sentence you write in the way I considered those above? No. But if you've never discovered through such analysis where your "style" resides, it would be a good idea to find out. Is your sentence length average 25 words, or 50? The difference between those two numbers also can mean the difference between readability and unreadability. Likewise, is the grade level of your writing the 10th grade, or the 20th grade (in other words, eight years of university education)? Is your Flesch Reading Ease score 60, or 30? All this information about your work can be yours with the click of a computer mouse. If you use Microsoft Word, it's probably available in your grammar checker software. (If you haven't seen a box containing sentence length information and readability indexes, you might find it through Word's "preferences.") Both Rudolf Flesch and Robert Gunning also have authored books containing readability indexes you can calculate "by hand"—that is, without computer software.

Again, the goal of these readability tools—as well as of these guidelines—is to craft prose so quick, silken, and natural that the reader understands it immediately and with a single reading. No need to go back and re-read. No need to take the work apart and put it together again in order to puzzle out the writer's intent. In other words, no need to do the *writer's* work. Much besides sentence length goes into that kind of readability, but other considerations aside, long, dense sentences always make fuzzy reading. For example:

> *In the present case, not until the final confrontation between Brigid and Sam in which Brigid, Sam's client, has been thoroughly unmasked as the liar and killer she is (that mystery solved), and the circumstances of Archer's death are revealed (the other mystery solved), is the story over, its central issue, the one that continued all the way from the beginning, satisfactorily tied up.*

Thirty-five words intervene between this sentence's keywords: *not until the final confrontation . . . is the story over.* If we cut the intervening words and hold them for later, we can write a clear declarative statement: *Not until the final confrontation between Brigid and Sam is the story over and its central issue resolved.* Thus condensed, even that tricky syntax is clear. But subject-verb-object word order brings the highest clarity: *The story isn't over until the final confrontation between Brigid and Sam resolves its central issue.*

Beyond its structural problems, though, that 64-word sentence is just too long. How might we condense and refine to make the sentence clear and readable? There's never just one way to rewrite a badly written passage, but clarifying the subject-verb-object relationship is one way:

> *The central issue in 'The Maltese Falcon' is not resolved until the final confrontation between Sam and his client, Brigid. That scene unmasks Brigid as a liar and killer, solves the mystery of Archer's death, and closes the story.*

Those two sentences, totaling 39 words, cut the passage almost in half but still say everything the original said—and say it so the reader understands at first reading.

Lists. One exception to this length guideline is a sentence containing a list. If the list is well crafted, the reader will be able to follow, whatever its length. Two practices will help you create clear and readable lists:

• Get subject and verb out of the way before embarking on the list (subject and verb will be in the words leading into the list, and the list will be the object of the verb. See the examples below.)

• Keep list items parallel (the first word of each list item will begin with the same part of speech). Here's an example of bad list-making:

> *All personnel functioning as salespeople must achieve the following to qualify for the Summit Club:*
>
> *Accounts Receivable Managers, Vendor Service Managers and Regional Vice Presidents who are in the position for nine months and achieve the sales goal for their portfolio sales, Segment Sales People who have been in the position for nine months and achieve 100 percent or more of quota, Regional Sales Managers who have been in the position for nine months and achieve 100 percent or more of quota by vendor location and Segment Coordinators who have been in the position for nine months and achieve 100 percent or more of quota in assigned segments will be eligible.*

That passage—a single sentence—is 111 words long. That still wouldn't be too long for a list if it were well executed. The elements in the list are parallel, but that "will be eligible" at sentence end comes as a shock. We had no idea while reading the list that we were headed for a verb. Even without that problem, the passage is unreadable because it's so dense and repetitive. A bulleted list would be easier to read and understand, and we need only three items or more for such a list. And where bulleted lists are appropriate, they are not only easy to execute, they also offer the reader white space, visual interest, and an orderly procession of ideas.

Revised:

The following sales staff members can qualify for the Summit Club. In all cases, candidates must have been their positions at least nine months.

- *Accounts receivable managers, vendor service managers, and regional vice presidents who reach their portfolio sale quotas*
- *Segment salespeople who reach or exceed their quotas*
- *Regional sales managers who reach or exceed their vendor location quotas*
- *Segment coordinators who reach or exceed assigned segment quotas*

The revised 74-word passage has been reduced by a third with no loss in information.

Consider this 91-word sentence from a city government memo:

The recommendations developed by the committee and contained in the plan attempt to take a very complex issue and enable the Smithfield community to conservatively address waste reduction goals and objectives in a cost-effective and environmentally sound manner. The plan examines the municipal solid waste stream, evaluates existing waste management practices, assesses community needs, identifies short and long-range management alternatives, coordinates the local solid waste activities with regional and state initiatives, and recommends a plan of action to encourage and achieve a greater degree of waste minimization, recycling, and resource recovery.

Length is not the only problem with this sentence, but it's the main one—coupled with the writer's not recognizing the opportunity of the bulleted list:

The committee's recommendations include inexpensive and environmentally sound ways to approach Smithfield's waste reduction goals. The plan:
- *examines the municipal solid-waste stream*
- *evaluates waste management practices*
- *assesses community needs*
- *identifies short- and long-range management alternatives*
- *coordinates local solid-waste activities with regional and state initiatives*
- *recommends ways to cut down waste and encourage recycling and resource recovery*

The revised version loses 30 unnecessary words, and it is clearer and more inviting in both content and appearance.

While the *bulleted* list is usually reserved for informational writing, there's no shortage of readable and interesting lists in creative or imaginative work—they're simply presented differently. Well-executed lists in creative fiction and nonfiction account for many stylish sentences that work despite their length. Charles Dickens often used lists to compress what might otherwise have been an overlong description (not that Dickens shrank from long descriptions!). Here's an example from *A Christmas Carol*:

Oh, but he was a tightfisted hand at the grindstone. Scrooge! a squeezing, wrenching, grasping, scraping, clutching, covetous old sinner! Hard and sharp as flint, from which no steel had ever struck out generous fire; secret, and self-contained, and solitary as an oyster.

John LeCarré has a sure hand with the riskiest material. Here's one of his stylish virtuoso performances, from *The Night Manager*. This imposing lot from international crime is "headed hungrily for the buffet":

After the Royals & Ancients came Burr's pet hates, and probably Roper's, too, for he called them the Necessary Evils.

These were the shiny-cheeked merchant bankers from London with eighties striped blue shirts and white collars and double-barreled names and double chins and double-breasted suits . . . . And in their train, the bully-boy accountants—the bean-counters, Roper called them—looking as though they'd come to extract a voluntary confession, with take-away curry breath and wet armpits and voices like formal cautions that from here on everything you say will be taken down and faked in evidence against you. And after them again, their non-British counter-parts: Mulder, the tubby notary from Curacao, with his twinkling smile and knowing waddle; Schreiber of Stuttgart, constantly apologizing for his ostentatiously good English; Thierry from Marseilles, with his pinched lips and toyboy secretary; the bond sellers from Wall Street, who never came in less than fours, as if there really were security in numbers; and Apostoll, the striving little Greek-American, with his toupee like a black bear's paw, his gold chains and gold crosses and unhappy Venezuelan mistress toppling uncomfortably behind him on her thousand-dollar shoes.

When does a list fail to work? At the beginning, when it hangs in a vacuum:

A marina at English Park. A floating or hanging walkway on the river stretching from Smothers Park to English Park. Turning First Street into a pedestrian mall downtown and a boulevard west of the Executive Inn. Those were among the ideas tossed out Wednesday at a . . . .

That poor beginning could be reclaimed if the writer set it up a bit:

A special city council meeting Wednesday that focused on improving the downtown area yielded some novel ideas: A marina at English Park. A floating or hanging walkway on the river stretching from Smothers Park to English Park. Turning

First Street into a pedestrian mall downtown and a boulevard west of the Executive Inn.

Keep to one idea per sentence: This doesn't mean to avoid simple main idea-subordinate-idea sentences—as long as both ideas together don't result in an unmanageable sentence. We write and speak in such sentences all the time: *I am going* (main idea), *but I don't want to* (subordinate idea). But try to figure out what is going on in the following 80-word sentence:

> *Many American travelers know St. Moritz, a jet-setting celebrity playground in southeast Switzerland, also as the two-time host of the Winter Olympics (1928 and 1948); as the birthplace (1864) of Alpine winter sports; as the chic resort that boasts of "sun and champagne climate"; as the 6,000-foot Upper Engadine lakeside setting for many Heidi books and movies, not to mention more intriguing themes, or perhaps even as the center of tiny Switzerland's fourth language (Romansch, after German, French and Italian).*

That writer throws so many ideas at us that we give up in disgust.

There's another and less common exception to this length guideline. Gifted writers of fiction or other creative work sometimes deliberately fashion a long sentence for certain stylistic reasons. That can work if the writer knows when and how to do it. (In technical writing, however, there's probably no reason to stretch sentence length beyond what bulleted lists can handle.) In any case, if you have legitimate reason to write a long sentence, be sure short ones surround it.

Here's a 74-word sentence from Tom Wolfe's *The Right Stuff* that would be awful if length were all that mattered. But Wolfe, known for his idiosyncratic but usually interesting style, keeps a tight rein on the sentence, and the reader is not lost.

The idea was to prove at every foot of the way up that you were one of the elected and anointed ones who had the right stuff and could move higher and higher and even—ultimately, God willing, one day—that you might be able to join that special few at the very top, that elite who had the capacity to bring tears to men's eyes, the very Brotherhood of the Right Stuff itself.

Compare Wolfe's sentence with the earlier sentence about St. Moritz, and you'll see the difference immediately. The St. Moritz sentence contains many wildly diverse ideas—some of them difficult or obscure ("Switzerland's fourth language, Romansch, after German, French and Italian"). The Wolfe sentence is of similar length but expands upon only one idea. Tom Wolfe begins: "The idea was"—and the rest of the sentence illuminates that idea. The sentence, although long, is simple in idea, execution, and vocabulary.

"To write simply," said W. Somerset Maugham, "is as difficult as to be good." In part, the long sentences above work because their words and ideas are simple and concrete. The next guideline will look at the hazards of turgid abstractions and imprecision.

CHAPTER 2

A Dozen Guidelines to Good Writing

Avoid Pretensions, Gobbledygook, and Euphemisms

Once precision is abandoned as a linguistic or literary virtue, vague generalization is one of the two remaining possibilities, gibberish being the second.

—Wendell Berry

I once spoke to a group of professional communicators about the hazards of pretentious mumbo jumbo in workplace writing. We talked about what happens when we use fuzzy but important-sounding language, or seek to impress rather than to communicate clearly and simply. An example:

> *Objective consideration of contemporary phenomena compels the conclusion that success or failure in competitive activities exhibits no tendency to be commensurate with innate capacity, but that a considerable element of the unpredictable must invariably be taken into account.*

We discussed that passage's reading level—well beyond 12th grade—and its readability index, a stunning 0.0. (Again, as mentioned in the last chapter, studies show that even the most educated Americans prefer to read at or below the 10th-grade reading level. The most common readability guide is the Flesch Reading Ease Index, which works on a 100-point scale. The higher the score, the easier the passage is to understand. An appropriate index for most writing is 60 to 70.)

Afterwards, a troubled professional who writes corporate publications—annual reports and the like—asked what she could do to "keep a foot in both camps." She meant one foot in clarity and simplicity and the other in bafflegab.

"Why would you want to?" I asked.

"Well, to keep our credibility with our more intelligent readers. We have to write for ma and pa on the farm, and we also have to please a highly educated audience."

What could I say? She misunderstands the face and function of simplicity. But so do a lot of people. When I was teaching university writing, one of my students declared another professor to be "brilliant" because that professor so seldom said anything she understood. And an engineer once complained that he was having a hard time getting his writing level above the 11th grade; he thought he would sound smarter if he "got a higher grade." But it was already too high! Again, most people prefer to read at or below the 10thgrade reading level. And that's no hardship; any decent writer or speaker can handle the most complex material at that level without "dumbing it down."

Let's put aside the notion that ma and pa won't understand anything very "intelligent"—the fact is that there isn't anything very *intelligent* about pretentious and abstract writing. To the contrary, one hallmark of intellect is the ability to simplify, to make the complex easy to understand. Anyone can be unclear.

The way to credibility is to speak and write plainly without language that bewilders or misleads. And the way to *lose* credibility is to veil the message in showy blather. Did Lincoln's audience at Gettysburg complain about the simplicity of his two-minute speech—a speech that still stands as a model of clarity and elegance?

Was Winston Churchill too clear when he said: "We shall fight on the beaches, we shall fight on the landing grounds, we shall fight in the fields and in the streets, we shall fight in the hills"? Would his more intelligent listeners have preferred to "engage in hostilities with incursive combatants in multiple locations"?

That passage in the second paragraph above with zero percent readability? It's George Orwell's deliberately turgid rewrite of a famous verse from Ecclesiastes:

> *I returned and saw under the sun, that the race is not to the swift, nor the battle to the strong, neither yet bread to the wise, nor yet riches to men of understanding, nor yet favor to men of skill; but time and chance happeneth to them all.*

That passage is beloved for its simplicity and deep meaning. Most of its words have one syllable; all are plain everyday words. It's written at the 8th-grade level and has a readability index of 78.3. Does Orwell's rewrite seem "smarter"? Would the intelligent reader prefer it?

Or does it turn out that what pleases ma and pa pleases us all?

Despite the obvious beauty and superiority of simplicity, dense and arcane phrasing seems to flourish everywhere. It's a particular problem in specialized fields—business, science, medicine, education, government, etc. It's as though we offer ourselves more latitude to write poorly when the subject is challenging. But that's the very time we must be at greater pains to simplify and clarify.

Someone in business might write, for example: "The CEO said that financial exigencies made it necessary for the company to implement budgetary measures to minimize expenditures." How would that sentence read if it were plain instead of fancy? *The CEO said the company had to cut costs.*

Turgid writing causes misunderstanding. When the message is obscured by verbal smog, the readers don't, in fact, *get* the message. They don't read, or they misread, or they misunderstand. The wasted time and effort as well as the cost of mistakes and misunderstanding make fuzzy writing an expensive habit wherever it flourishes. Given its cost, what explains the appeal of bloated, pretentious language? Or should I ask: "What elucidates the proliferation of indecipherable terminology and superfluous syllables"? How does "he left his car and ran" become "the perpetrator exited his vehicle and fled on foot"? How does a banana become an "elongated yellow fruit"?

We could probably do a dissertation on the answers. But it's enough to say that in trying to sound learned, to elevate our diction, we instead merely inflate it. Maybe we confuse simplicity with the over-simple. Maybe we think simplicity means "Run Dick Run." But simplicity is neither barren nor elementary; it is just immediately, attractively, interestingly *clear*.

A police chief told me that when he was an officer, he had to put together a report destined for the eyes of the city council. He was nervous about the task and wrote the report with dictionary and thesaurus at his elbow. He was proud of the result, which he thought sounded impressive, and was pleased when his superior and fellow officers said admiringly that they didn't know he "could write like that."

On city council day, a message came from the council members: They wanted to see the police officer who wrote the report. He went excitedly, expecting a slap on the back. Instead, the mayor waved the report at him and asked: "What does this mean?"

From then on, the chief added, "I always wrote in my own words."

Sometimes we slip into gobbledygook when we're trying to soften the message. Trying to make the message more palatable by manipulating the language sooner or later leads to euphemism, which at best amuses and at worst alienates. "That project lost money" becomes "that project had an adverse impact on anticipated revenue."

Euphemisms don't work. We all know by now that "collateral damage" means killing civilians. In a radio interview, a

Texas prison warden spoke not about rehabilitating the human beings within his walls, but about "creating functioning social units." One of the oddest and most transparent euphemisms I ever heard came from a personnel manager who spoke of "dehiring" an employee.

Clarity needn't—and shouldn't—mean brusque or rude. In any case, euphemistic gobbledygook does not soften. Rather, it makes readers suspicious—they wonder what the truth is behind those slippery words. Simple words seem more sincere and therefore soften best.

Turgid writing also can be an attempt to fudge. In an editing session, a writer once told me regarding a simple and direct revision of his opening paragraphs: "If I'm going to be that clear, I'd also better be that right."

Being "that right" is always part of the writer's job.

Should we avoid all long words and abstractions? No. It wouldn't be desirable even if it were possible. As Albert Einstein advised: "Everything should be made as simple as possible, but not simpler." A long word is the right word if it's the *best* word. What damages clarity is piling up long and abstract words when short and concrete words are readily available. It's writing "utilization" instead of *use*. Or "pursuant to" instead of *concerning* or *regarding*. Or "indicate" instead of *say, show*, or *suggest*. It's "initiate" and "terminate" instead of *begin* and *end*, or "contingent upon" instead of *depends on*, "personal visitation" instead of *visit*, "telephonic communication" instead of *phone call*. It's "financial wherewithal" for *money*, "funding" instead of *funds*, "programming" instead of *programs*.

Jargon and buzz phrases also make meaning slip away:

> *This equity account was not immune to the effects of the market's negative growth because of its broad, benchmark-centric investment approach.*

Or: *This fund lost money*. Or, more specifically: *This fund is down almost 60 percent.* The linguistic travesty "negative growth" is a contradiction in terms that actually means *decrease, reduction,* or *decline*—growth that is "negative" is not growth at all. Writers who pass on such euphemisms are not doing readers a favor.

The passage also misleads in its ploy of saying what something is *not* rather than what it is. The fund was "not immune." Sounds relatively benign. In fact, the fund was ravaged. And "broad, benchmark-centric investment approach" *sounds* impressive. We just don't know what it means.

An illogical "advance" or "pre" tacked onto words that should stand alone is favored in the world of jargon—*advance planning* or *preplanning, advance warning* or *prewarning,* for example. (All planning and warning must be done in advance.) The airlines' *preboard* is a special oddity. How do you get on the plane before you get on the plane?

George Orwell, who considered abstractions not just unpleasantly unclear but dangerous if they masked the truth, said: "Modern writing at its worst does not consist in picking out words for the sake of their meaning and inventing images in order to make the meaning clearer. It consists in gumming together long strips of words which have already been set in order by someone else, and making the results presentable by sheer humbug."

How can we sidestep the snare of the pretension? As writers, we must stop admiring and mimicking meaningless language and buzz phrases. We must stop trying to impress and try instead to *communicate*—heaven knows that's hard enough. In part, that means disabusing ourselves of the notion that big words "sound" better—more intelligent, more professional, more serious. We'll seek concrete rather than abstract phrasing. We'll use only with restraint such abstract nouns as *condition, process, nature, issue, case, question, facility, factor, basis, nature.* Consider the following: The condition of his health is a problem. *He's in poor health.* The clean-up at the federal facility will be a slow process. *The federal building clean-up will be slow.* They submitted a proposal of a questionable nature. *They submitted a questionable proposal.* They're pondering the childcare issue. *They're pondering childcare.*

The following passage is from a company considering moving into computer leasing:

> *Today, technological advances and business needs change at an explosive pace. These changes force technological obsolescence, depreciate equipment values and create the risks associated with asset ownership. Companies are in the precarious position of balancing the desire to take advantage of current and future technologies with the need to maintain a high level of equipment usage on a cost-effective basis. Traditional patterns of equipment ownership do not meet corporate objectives.*

Notice that this overblown passage, written by a member of the company's public relations staff, never uses the words *computer* or *lease.* When I pointed this out to the writer, whose work his company asked me to critique, he was shocked and disbelieving. When he saw for himself, however, that he had left out the very words that would best clarify and persuade, he said glumly that he had apparently lost the ability to communicate. But he hadn't. Orally, he communicated perfectly well— clearly, simply, and interestingly.

How does this happen? How does a professional writer forget how to speak on paper? In many cases, it's because of workplace jargon and abstraction, buzz phrases that sound important and say little.

How could we rewrite the passage above to make it immediately clear, concrete, warm, and meaningful? First, let's consider the passage in detail:

Today: The reader assumes we're talking about "today"; no need to sound like a proclamation. *At an explosive pace* is the same thing as "explosively," which, although shorter, is an overused adverb. *These changes force technological obsolescence, depreciate equipment values and create the risks associated with asset ownership:* Whew, a mouthful. And what does it *mean*—especially "asset ownership"? *Companies are in the precarious position of balancing the desire to take advantage of current and future technologies:* What is the "precarious position" companies are in? That of balancing a *desire* with a *need*. That's tricky enough, but what is that need? To "take advantage of current and future technologies" and to "maintain a high level of equipment usage on a cost-effective basis." First, that "future"—how does one "take advantage of" technology that isn't yet developed? Second, what is the company maintaining a high level of? *Equipment usage.* Does "a high level of usage" mean heavy use? Does "a cost-effective basis" mean inexpensive? What does not meet corporate objectives? *Traditional patterns.* Even worse: traditional patterns of *equipment ownership.* Is ownership a *pattern,* traditional or otherwise? Doesn't "patterns of ownership" simply mean *ownership?*

The big question in rewriting dense and fuzzy passages is the writer's meaning. Sometimes it takes some digging to discover the embedded message, but once it's unearthed, you'll find it's nearly always simple rather than complex. That's the case here. There's never just one way to rewrite a passage, but here's one version:

> *Rapid advances in technology have made it impractical for businesses to buy computer systems. Since expensive equipment depreciates overnight and becomes outdated while still new, owning that equipment can mean loss of both money and productivity. Leasing computers can be cheaper and more efficient, however, because a company can add and upgrade without the cost of ownership.*

That version uses concrete words and—as we'll discuss more fully in the next chapter—it also reduces the *size* of the words where it can. Short, familiar words promote concrete expression. Short words are small, strong, and suited to story telling; long words are bulky, weak, and suited (often with unfortunate results) to report writing.

Would a storyteller say: "He manifested displeasure as he gained access to his domicile"? No, the storyteller would say: "He scowled as he came into the house." But as we've seen, small words also benefit the complex and specialized worlds of informational writing. We should trust them more.

CHAPTER 3

A Dozen Guidelines to Good Writing

Change Long and Difficult Words to Short and Simple Words

Short words are best and the old words when short are best of all.
—Winston Churchill

Early in my university teaching career, I agreed to teach basic or remedial English one night a week to special-needs students, many of whom were itinerant farm laborers who spoke English as a second language. The students were of varied backgrounds but of similar zeal: Each had paid for 16 weeks of instruction. Because it was a university extension course, tuition was nominal compared to that of a college credit course, but it was still expensive for people who labored seasonally for minimum wages.

Because of their commitment and enthusiasm, those students did well, but in one important way, they taught me more than I taught them.

Throughout the class, the students kept a daily journal. I saw it as a sort of loosening up, a relaxation exercise. They wrote in their journals anything they wished, but for at least 30 minutes a day—and I collected, read, commented upon, and corrected them monthly.

Those journals were an education. I watched the students become better writers, not so much because they were getting instruction in grammar and structure—although that helped—but because they grew more comfortable and confident. They became, at least on paper, more fully themselves. Some of them had fretted at the beginning of the semester that they didn't have the vocabulary to write. Never mind, I said, use the vocabulary you have. I told them of Joseph Conrad, who came to English late, then wrote it more imaginatively and suggestively than many who spoke it as a mother tongue. He once wrote, for example, of returning to his ship when he heard an explosion on board: "I *swarmed* up the rope." Native English speakers probably would not think of writing *swarmed* as something one person could do, but it was a fine word for the context because it conjured up a frenzy of arms and legs.

I told the students to write quickly, without consulting dictionary or thesaurus while they were writing—although they might do so later. I told them not to go back and rewrite or correct anything, that I was not grading the journals, and that to get credit, all they had to do was write.

In short, it was to be a stress-free exercise, something to get them writing and to lay the groundwork for more complex work.

At first, their journals were mostly artificial and self-conscious, written for show. I could tell they were trying to impress, and reading and commenting on the writing was no fun. But over time, the journals became increasingly basic and honest—and increasingly beautiful and accurate. Here's a sentence from one of those journals: "My mom didn't have much school and when I told her I signed up for this, she drew her eyes down thin and squeezed her lips."

That sentence has much going for it, and the proof is that I never forgot it. As I read *she drew her eyes down thin*, I realized most of us would write: "she narrowed her eyes"; for *squeezed her lips,* most of us would write: "she pursed her lips." Yet this young writer's description was somehow fresher and more real because she didn't know the "code." English was not her mother tongue—she simply described what she saw with the words she had.

The writing in that class of "special needs" students often had a marked and somehow indefinable beauty. I thought at the time that it was the natural beauty of simplicity. But that was only partly right. I'd missed an important feature of their work, one I would come later to understand.

Eventually, I began to do "timed writing" and free association exercises in writing workshops. I'd give the writers a little time—ten minutes at most—and an opening fragment. When I said *go*, they finished the fragment and continued writing, without stopping and as fast as they could. The idea was to fill up as much space with words as possible in the short time they had.

That writing task was chiefly a freeing exercise, as the student journals had been, and again, I noticed something revelatory: The resulting writing was nearly always excellent—clear, conversational, storytelling. This was true even of professional writers who typically wrote about complicated subjects and whose styles tended to be dense and unreadable.

It was while admiring one such writer's work that I had a sudden realization: Nearly all the words were one-syllable words, and the few that were not were still simple and familiar. I started thumbing through the exercises with increasing excitement. It was true of all the work.

I added single-syllable writing exercises to my bag of workshop tasks and since then have seen hundreds of examples. I have never read *bad* one-syllable writing. The weakest is good; the best is excellent, even fine. The certain beauty I'd noticed in that long-ago class was commonplace in single-syllable writing.

Why is this? What is the special magic of the small word?

Many of our most ancient words are one-syllable utterances. Such words tend to be concrete and emotive, involving the senses: *earth, sun, sky, star, cloud, wind, rain, snow, food, drink, smell, taste, sound, sight, feel*. If an old, plain word is a "concept" word, its concept is usually familiar and, again, emotive rather than abstract: *life, death, love, hate, war, peace*. Among the most familiar and concrete words are those we carry around with us all the time—our bodies. From *head* to *toe,* we have *skin* and *bone: face, brow, eye, nose, lip, mouth, teeth, tongue, throat, cheek, jaw, chin, ear, neck, chest, breast, back, spine, arm, wrist, hand, hip, leg, knee, thigh, calf, foot* . . . . And, yes, we have *shoulder, elbow, ankle,* and *finger*—not to mention *intestine, appendix,* and other polysyllabic gear. But you get the point: The stuff we know best usually has a simple name.

The clearest, most stirring writers and speakers depend upon plain, short words, and those words often create a moving blend of clarity, simplicity, and dignity. Also, short words usually don't go to war with each other; they have a nice mesh. There's a wealth of example. The King James Version of the Holy Bible is filled with short words, from its first lines to its last:

Beginning: *In the beginning God created the heaven and the earth. And the earth was without form, and void; and darkness was upon the face of the deep. And the Spirit of God moved upon the face of the waters. And God said let there be light: and there was light.*

End: *The grace of our Lord Jesus Christ be with you all. Amen.*

Or think of the words of memorable speakers and writers: Winston Churchill: "Blood, toil, tears, and sweat." "To jaw-jaw is always better than to war-war." Franklin Delano Roosevelt: "Never before have we had so little time in which to do so much." "The only thing we have to fear is fear itself." Abraham Lincoln:

> *I do the very best I know how—the very best I can; and I mean to keep doing so until the end. If the end brings me out all right, what is said against me won't amount to anything. If the end brings me out wrong, ten angels swearing I was right would make no difference.*

Shakespeare had a huge vocabulary for his time and was well able to adorn his work not only with arcane and showy expression but also with popular Latinisms. For the most riveting moments, however, he chose the simplest phrasing: "My heart is turned to stone; I strike it, and it hurts my hand." "Let's carve him as a dish fit for the gods, not hew him as a carcass fit for hounds." "All the world's a stage, and all the men and women merely players." "To be or not to be: that is the question." "He wears the rose of youth upon him." "As flies to wanton boys, are we to the gods, they kill us for their sport." "We are such stuff as dreams are made on, and our little life is rounded with a sleep."

Churchill. Roosevelt. Lincoln. Shakespeare. Not one of them ever felt like saying "It is axiomatic that the assumption of linearity in combinations is not legitimate for composite calibrations."

Chief Joseph's speech to the Nez Percé tribe after surrendering in the 1877 battle of Bear Paw Mountains has touched readers for a century and a quarter for its dignity, simplicity, and clarity. An excerpt:

> *My people, some of them have run away to the hills and have no blankets, no food. No one knows where they are, perhaps freezing to death. I want to have time to look for my children and see how many of them I can find. Maybe I can find them among the dead. Hear me, my chiefs. My heart is sick and sad. From where the sun now stands, I will fight no more forever.*

In that deeply affecting 76-word passage, 66 words have one syllable. All but one of the rest are simple two-syllable words: *people, away, blankets, perhaps, freezing, children, many, among.* The passage's final word is the lone three-syllable word, but it couldn't be simpler. And it resonates sadly long after the period: *forever.*

For several years, I led a committee on writing and editing for the Associated Press Managing Editors association. That committee, part of a continuing studies effort, was made up of editors and educators from across the country. In part, we researched and distributed to the association's membership yearly reports concerning writing and editing.

For one such report, we asked high school English teachers in a small Midwestern town to assign to their students a one-syllable writing exercise. Here are several excerpts from those essays, with thanks to the teachers and students of Rensselaer (Indiana) Central High:

When I stepped through the rocks to glimpse the coast for the first time in my life, I was awed. The wide blue sea glowed with light from the sun, and wisps of smooth white clouds soared in the huge, free sky. A boat, far out at sea, dipped in the waves, and small white gulls hung in the sky as if they had no weight. The waves, topped with foam, lapped at the rocks. I took off my shoes and ran on the rough, wet sand at the edge of the sea. It was cold and clear and sent a chill up my back. I walked a long time. I could feel the rays of sun beat on my skin, and I was warm and tired. There were few sounds, just the waves and the gulls.

Now I am on the top of the first slope of the year. I push off and plunge down the slope. I hear the cuts of ice on the steel edge of a ski. Then there's a swoosh sound of snow. On the side of the hill I see a drift of snow and ski to it. The drift shoots me through the air high above the heads of those next to me. The flight in the air seems long and smooth.

It was a nice day on the beach. There was a breeze, and the sky was blue and clear. A bird with quick feet ran down the beach and flew up near a kite with a long piece of string that a child held in his small hands. It swayed through the sky and swooped down toward an old man with a wide-brimmed straw hat on his head.

We see in those examples that "certain beauty" I mentioned earlier. Because the passages are descriptive rather than expository writing, that sense of beauty is heightened. But the clarity that comes with honest, basic expression benefits all writing. Utter simplicity offers the bedrock of authenticity. In some ways, one-syllable writing is an attempt to get at the truth.

That's what Ernest Hemingway meant when he said he'd spent the whole of his writing career trying to find "one true word." Gustave Flaubert echoed that sentiment, as have many other writers who are celebrated for fine craft. The brilliant writer and thinker Bertrand Russell even joked about it: "I am paid by the word," he said, "so I always write the shortest words possible."

Despite the obvious superiority of simple language, writers sometimes fear that small words might suggest their vocabularies are small and simple as well. "What's the use of knowing lots of fancy words," they fret, "if you're not going to use them?" We can consider that notion the Diamond Jim Brady theory of communication. James Brady was an American financier and philanthropist in the 1800s. He rose from humble beginnings to amass a fortune selling for a railroad supply company and investing his profits. But money didn't nullify his crude beginnings. Diamond Jim became known—and named—for his tasteless display of jewelry. When asked why he was so bedecked with gems, he is said to have responded: "Them as has 'em wears 'em."

The newly rich Brady didn't understand the fallacy of ostentatious display (excess is vulgar) or the paradox of good taste (less is more). Good taste shows restraint and simplicity: Them as has 'em wears just one or two—but the *right* one or two. The rest stay in the safe for another occasion.

It's the same with words. Owning many words informs and enriches our communication even when we leave most of them in the safe. And the more words we know, the surer and freer we are to choose the plainest, simplest—and *right*—words. After all, having knowledge is useful only if we can convey it clearly and briefly—and that means translating the complex into the simple. That can't happen when we write, as Virginia Woolf said, "as if thought plunged into a sea of words and came up dripping."

Should you get serious about all this? Should you try to use only one-syllable words? By all means get serious about it. But using only one-syllable words would be impossible even if it were desirable. Capitalized words will always be exempt, for example. And sometimes the shortest word is not the most *accurate* word. A professional writer who was doing one-syllable exercises once said, "I'm writing about creosote. Should I call it *tar*?" No, call it *creosote*; that's what it is, and that's its accurate and most meaningful label.

In the passage below, how can we sensibly reduce *contribution, reimburse,* or *volunteered*? We probably can't. And there's no need to if we shorten the words we can. *Contribution, policy,* and *reimburse* are familiar and easy to understand unless—as these are—they're caught in a thicket of wordiness and abstraction.

> *Departmental regulations at 45 CFR Part 74, Subpart G, allow the value of in-kind contributions to count toward grantee cost sharing. However, regulations at 42 CFR 430.30(e) specifically exclude the Medicaid program from these Department regulations. The regulations implementing the 1991 statute on donations and taxes do not alter the fundamental policy that allows reimbursement only of allowable expenses the State actually incurs. Therefore, the value of the volunteered hours would not be eligible for Federal Financial Participation.*

Here's that passage rewritten into shorter words wherever we can do so with benefit: "In-kind contributions count toward cost-sharing in some cases [45 CFR Part 74, Subpart G]. But Medicaid is excluded [42 CFR 430.30(e)]. We reimburse only actual costs the state incurs. The value of volunteered hours is not eligible for federal matching because the state incurred no costs."

That's a difficult technical passage, but as you see from the rewrite, even difficult technical material can be relatively easy to understand if the writer is determined to make it so. Even simple ideas slip away, however, when they're unnecessarily told in long words: "At Acme, our ability to execute the company's strategic mission is critically dependent upon developing approaches that allow us to fulfill difficult and mutable federal requirements." Those long words do nothing to promote precision; they merely obscure meaning. If we shorten them, a simple idea emerges: "We must find ways to meet tough and changing federal requirements if we're to reach company goals."

We live in a complex world, and we sometimes must use complex words. We use those words when they're the best or only words for the context. But if—*whenever we have a choice*—we choose the shortest words, we'll create a clear and simple setting for those necessary complications, and long words will damage our writing less.

But don't expect it to be easy; it's harder than it looks. Because of their natural readability, short words seem effortless. That's deceptive. As author and educator Jacques Barzun said, "Simple English is no one's mother tongue. It has to be worked for."

CHAPTER 4

Be Wary of Jargon, Fad, and Cliché

The original writer is not one who imitates nobody, but one whom nobody can imitate.
> —François René de Chateaubriand

When I was in grad school working on my thesis, I would sometimes be asked at a party: *What are you studying?* I would say something like: *Essentially myth and archetypal criticism. I'm focusing on the image in literature of the Great Mother.* Now, I didn't roll my eyes or waggle my brow as I said this. I didn't speak sardonically from the corner of my mouth, or elbow anyone in the ribs. I was *serious*, even earnest.

Did I see their eyes glaze? Did I notice their bewildered expressions? I did. And I did not know why.

What was my problem? I'd lived so closely within a narrow field of study that I'd lost sight of how very narrow it was. I'd forgotten that most of the world didn't know or give a darn about archetypal criticism, whatever that was, or the Great Mother, whoever she was. I had breathed rarefied air so long I had oxygen debt.

That often happens with ungoverned jargon.

Is all jargon all bad all the time? By no means. Fact is, as the world and our knowledge of it becomes more segmented and specialized, so does the language. I might be lost at a meeting of the American Medical Association, but physicians would not be. Imagine the great blot of words it would take to explain highly specialized material to a non-specialized audience. But if the audience shares that certain specialty, writers shouldn't even try—that audience knows the terms and expects them. Take a small and simple bit of jargon—*signage*.

To someone involved in, say, a city transportation department, that little word carries big meaning. It means the whole subject of signs: deciding where they go, how they should look, what they should say, ordering them, paying for them, installing them. A lay person might ask: *Is that even a word?* And the answer is *yes*. It is a word to the specialist who understands it, and it's an exceptionally useful and meaningful word—a brief way to say much.

That's *good* jargon—a specialized term for a similarly specialized audience. The challenge for the communicator is imparting specialized knowledge and insights to the rest of the world. That means translating good jargon into plain English for a lay audience. The following passage, taken from an employee newspaper brief, shows what happens when specialized jargon is not translated:

> *Recent enhancements to the Voluntary Personal Accident Insurance and Accidental Death and Dismemberment plans include increased coverage for paraplegia and hemiplegia insurance and the addition of spouse vocational training benefits and double benefits for dismembered children.*

That insurance jargon would be OK if the readers were insurance specialists rather than lay readers. The writer, from the company's human resources department, has probably been exposed to this sort of language so much that it sounds like English to him. But it doesn't to others. How might this passage have been written with the lay reader in mind?

> *The company has increased insurance for accident victims. The new plan increases benefits for employees who suffer paralysis of both legs or of one side of the body as a result*

of an accident. It also provides for spouse training and doubles benefits for children who lose a limb.

Again, good communication means imparting specialized knowledge and insights to the non-specialized world—and that means translating jargon into English so that the message is clear to all.

That's what I forgot with my party blather about archetypal criticism. Yet it wouldn't have been blather to my grad school colleagues—it would have been good jargon. That's why the frequently heard admonition "Avoid jargon!" is less than helpful—it goes both too far and not far enough. Such an admonition is simply too sweeping unless it really means—as it usually does—to avoid *bad* jargon. Not all specialized language is good; some is unnecessary, unclear, virtually meaningless, and advanced for the wrong reasons. That's bad communication wherever you find it.

Take the following passage from a guest column in a newspaper:

> *Wolves are wide-ranging and any attempts to short-circuit that results in threats to the wolf populations either from anthropogenic actions or from a variety of stochastic environmental perturbations.*

That passage means that restricting the wolves' habitat could also reduce their numbers, either by human or random environmental disturbance. It's nobody's "good jargon." Good jargon is expression that sets forth the complex in economical, albeit specialized, language. Bad jargon is expression that sets forth the simple in bloated language. The problem is that bad jargon—in the same way that euphemism often covers lies—often covers inanities. It's not that we can't and don't make foolish statements without jargon, but without jargon, the audience usually knows they're foolish. Wrapped in the bafflegab of jargon, inanities can actually sound *smart*. That's *sham*—always hurtful to good communication.

We dealt with pretensions in Chapter 2 and need say here only that pretensions accompany and account for much bad jargon. And much jargon arises from "buzz" words.

A buzz word is a word that taken alone might be both clear and meaningful but slips into meaningless "buzz" when accompanied by other buzz words. Here's such a passage:

> *We can unify this approach by optimizing our material dollars and resolving issues with regard to variances in our process capability results. We utilize this framework to generate and communicate direction, accomplished through our strategic planning process as well as through an annual procedure which helps to set organizational priorities. Goals must be established and deployed to provide consistency across the organization and to augment the supporting elements of structure and roles and responsibilities.*

That passage typifies buzz words. The phrasing is usually noun heavy, as in "process capability results." The reader can understand such words alone but is confused when they are together. Below are common buzz words:

capitalization
components
deployment
elements
facility
functionality
incentivation
indices
input
integration
interface
leverage
logistical
matrices

mechanism
operational
optimal
optimize
optimum
paradigm shift
parameters
preassessment
prioritization
procedure
process
remediation
stage
phase
level
strategic, strategize
synergy
system
utilization, utilize

Here's a little game that shows how buzz phrases work: Try putting together several of the above words until you have something that sounds like it means something—"system remediation integration," for example. Then remix the same words: "remediation integration system." Or "integration system remediation." Each combination will be equally highfalutin—and equally meaningless.

Hackneyed media writing is also a particular jargon problem partly because everyone is exposed to it, and partly because media writers are probably the only specialists who don't *speak* the jargon they write—which only shows how unconversational it is. Here's a miscellany of worn-out media lingo:

amid
arguably
beleaguered

bloody coup
bottom line
bottomed out
brought under fire
burgeoning
cautious optimism
chilling effect
cries of protest
critical mass
cutting edge
decimate
defining moment
delegate-rich
drew fire
dynasty (sports)
economic crunch
embattled
eponymous
escalated
escalating conflict
facility
famously
freefall
ground zero
hammered out
hard line
heated debate
heated exchange
heightened criticism
held hostage
hot line
hotly contested
in the wake of
infrastructure
jump start
laundry list

level the playing field
litany
looking to
low profile
mushroom
oil-rich
on the ground
on the upswing
political football
political suicide
reeling
resonate
send a message
send a signal
sharp decrease
skyrocketing
soft line
spark
spawn
spur
staggering
staunch defense
steep decline
strife-torn
stunning
sudden downturn
surprise move
sweeping
thin line
unleash a new round
unprecedented
venue
wide-ranging
widespread violence
witch hunt
worst-case scenario

Faddish expression and clichés are related. Borrowed from anywhere and everywhere, new and old, some words and expressions suddenly and often inexplicably catch fire. Someone says "at the end of the day" instead of *finally* or *ultimately*, and in no time at all, a million other someones are intoning *at the end of the day*. Sometimes a new expression will stick and become part of the lexicon; more often fads die away with a whisper. Does anyone want to hear "awesome" or "duh" anymore?

The problem with language fad and cliché is obvious: Over time, such expression grows flat, predictable, and dull. Mimicry is the antithesis of freshness and originality in all craft and art, and communication is no exception.

Here are some much-hated words and expressions that are nevertheless enjoying at least 15 minutes of undeserved fame:

closure
cobble together
cusp
empowerment
got game
has a problem with
has issues
having said that
impact (as a verb)
litmus test
make no mistake about it
material breach
mental toughness
push the envelope
raise the bar
ramp up
ratchet up
rush to judgment
that said
window of opportunity
24-7

In other (less than fresh) words, you don't have to be a brain surgeon or rocket scientist to know that fadspeak is the language from hell, or our worst nightmare. I mean: been there, done that. Even the totally clueless know it's just yadda, yadda, yadda, the same old same old. Don't even go there. It's history. A no-brainer. You think people really want to hear "just doesn't get it" or "get a life" or "yeah, right"? Oh, puhleeze, in your dreams. It's so *over*.

I'm outta here.

CHAPTER 5

A Dozen Guidelines to Good Writing

Use the Right Word

The difference between the right word and the nearly right word is the same as the difference between lightning and the lightning bug.

—Mark Twain

Consider the phrasing in these two advertisements: This product is the "penultimate" and that drink has a richer, more "fulsome" flavor."

Oops.

Neither of those ads says what it intends. *Penultimate* derives from Latin roots that mean "almost ultimate"—in other words, almost the end, or *next to last*. The next-to-last batter in the lineup is the *penultimate* batter, whatever his skills. Those who wrote that ad copy must have thought the word meant "extra" ultimate, or the absolute ultimate. But how could that be? How could anything be *more* than ultimate? That's like being "extra" pregnant or "completely" decapitated or "very" unique.

And *fulsome*. Does it mean full, lavish, or abundant, as seems to be the suggestion in this ad? It does not. Or at least it has not since the 16th century. The accepted meaning of *fulsome* is "disgusting" or "offensive." Surely the advertisers didn't mean that their drink had a disgusting or offensive flavor.

Penultimate and *fulsome* are two widely misunderstood words, and if they continue to be misused—first by many, then by *most*—their "accepted" definitions will also shift.

The accepted definition of *fortuitous*, for example, is by chance or accident—not "fortunate." But because that word is widely misunderstood, some dictionaries have added "fortunate" as an "alternate" meaning. The purpose of a dictionary is to help the reader discern what someone might have meant by a given word. Dictionaries are more *de*scriptive than *pre*scriptive. They generally don't try to say what is right, just what *is*. Many include usage notes where they can, but obviously space constraints apply—they have their work cut out for them simply dealing with the huge English lexicon.

In other words, definitions are not like grammar, which changes very little if at all. Usage is not so much a matter of *right and wrong* as it is *acceptable and questionable*. William Safire was correct when he said about word use: "When enough of us are wrong, we're right." Words finally must mean what most educated readers think they mean. Definitions are not set in stone. Perceptions change and, over time, some words change to match that perception, and dictionary committees will sooner or later add the new meaning as a possible definition. In time, the new definition may overtake the old and become the accepted (some say "preferred") definition. Again, that's the dictionary's job— to reflect current understanding.

But word change is slow and uncertain, and for the sake of clarity and credibility, it's best to stick to accepted definitions. How we use words matters if only because we may be judged ignorant (by some) for what they consider a misuse. In short, every serious writer should own several respected and up-to-date dictionaries as well as a good reference work on usage.

Here's a little quiz that presents frequently misused and misunderstood words. The answers, which follow, chiefly present accepted definitions. I consulted a variety of works in compiling this list, and the answers largely reflect unanimous opinion. The relatively permissive Webster's New World Dictionary was the final arbiter in the rare dispute.

Following the quiz is a list of tricky word pairs.

1. podium
a. platform sandal
b. stand that speakers place their notes on
c. platform that speakers stand on
d. foot doctor

2. epitome
a. embodiment
b. peak
c. perfect
d. core

3. friable
a. easily crumbled
b. withered
c. frizzy
d. monkish

4. decimate
a. to use decimals
b. to destroy a fraction
c. to destroy all
d. to marry in December

5. flout
a. disregard
b. flounder
c. show off
d. whip

6. gauntlet
a. narrow lane between two lines
b. medieval whip
c. musical scale
d. glove

7. disinterested

a. exhausted

b. annoyed

c. bored

d. unbiased

8. antebellum

a. auspicious

b. before the war

c. against bells

d. form of belladonna

9. restive

a. peaceful

b. thoughtful

c. fidgety, resisting control

d. relaxed

10. prone

a. lying face down

b. pertaining to the ankle bones

c. dead

d. lying face up

11. reticent

a. reluctant

b. silent

c. whimsical

d. nasal

12. tortuous

a. lawsuit

b. causing pain

c. flat bread

d. winding

13. ingenuous
a. dishonest
b. hypocritical
c. guileless
d. imaginative

14. votary
a. vestment
b. voting box
c. polling place
d. one bound by a vow

15. aquiline
a. like an eagle
b. turquoise
c. an aquarium lining
d. underwater movement

Answers

1. **podium** *c.* a platform that speakers stand upon. Frequently confused with *lectern* or *rostrum*, behind which speakers stand and place their notes.
2. **epitome** *a.* embodiment. *Epitome* means an abridgment or summary—not an *ideal*.
3. **friable** *a.* easily crumbled
4. **decimate** *b.* to destroy or remove a fraction of. Literally, 10 percent.
5. **flout** *a.* To disregard or hold in contempt, as in *flout the law,* or *flout convention*. Sometimes confused with *flaunt,* to show off or display.
6. **gauntlet** *d.* glove. We run the gamut or gantlet, but throw down the gauntlet—as in issuing a challenge (once, to challenge to a duel). Often confused with *gantlet,* originally a punishment in which the victim had to run between two rows of people who beat him.
7. **disinterested** *d.* unbiased

8. **antebellum** *b.* before the war
9. **restive** *c.* fidgety, resisting control
10. **prone** *a.* lying face down
11. **reticent** *b.* silent
12. **tortuous** *d.* winding, as in a crooked or twisting road; also, by extension, deceitful. Often confused with *torturous*, meaning to cause or inflict pain.
13. **ingenuous** *c.* guileless
14. **votary** *d.* one bound by a vow, as a monk or nun. Also, by extension, a devotee or enthusiast.
15. **aquiline** *a.* like an eagle, as in an "aquiline nose," meaning like an eagle's beak.

Tricky word pairs

This brief lexicon calls attention to frequently confused word pairs. It's not meant to be exhaustive, but suggestive. The list has bare-bones definitions, presenting chief and accepted definitions in general language and offering alternate meanings and further explanation only when necessary. For fuller treatments and extended definitions, consult a dictionary.

abjure, adjure
abjure: disavow, renounce
adjure: to place [someone] under oath
abrogate, arrogate
abrogate: to abolish or annul
arrogate: to claim or seize without right; to ascribe without reason
affect, effect
affect: influence, impress, touch, sway (the weather affected our decision; the film was deeply affecting). Or: artificial, pretentious (he is affected: he affects a British accent; his British accent is an affectation).

effect, noun: consequence, result, outcome (the movie had quite an effect on me); verb: to result in or bring about (the economy has effected a change in company policy).

allude, elude

allude: to refer to

elude: to escape or evade

all right, alright

all right is the accepted form; most experts consider *alright* a misspelling.

a lot, alot

a lot is the accepted form; avoid *alot*.

awhile, a while

awhile: adverb meaning for a brief time (sit down and stay *awhile*).

a while: noun meaning an indefinite time (we haven't been there for *a while*). Uses the preposition *for* or another preposition such as *in*.

bate, bait

bate: to reduce in force or intensity, to restrain (as in bated breath)

bait, noun: a lure; verb: to lure

balky, bulky

balky: uncooperative, contrary

bulky: big, having bulk, unwieldy

boast, boost

boast: to brag

boost, verb: to support or promote; noun: a push (they gave him a boost).

bruit, brute

bruit: to noise abroad, to spread rumor

brute: beast

bus, buss

bus: vehicle

buss: kiss

callus, callous

callus: thickened layer of skin

callous: cold, cruel, insensitive

closure, cloture

closure, noun: something that closes or shuts; verb: the act of closing

cloture: a vote of Congress to end a filibuster

compliment, complement

compliment: flattering remark

complement: to complete; counterpart

comprise, consist, constitute

Comprise means to include or contain and is used the way those words are used. Avoid *comprise of*. (*Consist* takes *of*; *comprise* doesn't.) The whole *comprises* the parts. This is a nation *comprising* 50 states. That set of history books *comprises* 30 volumes. But: The whole *consists of* the parts. The parts *constitute* the whole

condemn, contemn

condemn: to criticize strongly or judge unfit for

contemn: to treat with contempt, look down on

defuse, diffuse

defuse: to remove or make safe an explosive device; metaphorically, to calm (the speaker defused the situation)

diffuse, verb: to spread, scatter, or distribute widely; adjective: wordy, rambling

demur, demure

demur: to take exception to

demure: modest, shy

depreciate, deprecate

depreciate: to reduce or lose value; more rarely, to disparage. (Some object to the latter sense as confusing, and confused with *deprecate*.)

deprecate: to criticize or belittle

disburse, disperse

disburse: to pay out

disperse: to scatter

discomfit, discomfort

discomfit: to thwart or frustrate

discomfort: to make uncomfortable, distress

discreet, discrete

discreet: prudent or reserved in conduct or speech

discrete: separate, individually distinct

elicit, illicit

elicit: evoke, draw forth

illicit: unlawful, disapproved by society

emigrate, emigrant, immigrate, immigrant

emigrate, emigrant: to leave one's country and settle elsewhere; one who leaves one's country and settles elsewhere (he emigrated from China)

immigrate, immigrant: to come to and settle in a new country; one who comes to and settles in a new country (he immigrated to the United States)

envelop, envelope

envelop: to enclose or surround

envelope: a wrapping or cover, as for a letter

exult, exalt

exult: to rejoice in

exalt: to glorify

exercise, exorcise

exercise, verb: to use, apply, or employ; noun: fitness workout

exorcise: to purify or drive out evil spirits

farther, further

farther: go beyond a certain point, refers to literal distance (go farther down the street)

further: go beyond a certain point, refers to figurative distance (give it further thought)

flack, flak

flack: press agent

flak: antiaircraft gunfire; criticism or censure

forego, forgo

forego: to go before

forgo: to abstain from or give up

forte (French), forte (Italian)

forte (French), noun: strong point or suit, specialty; pronounced FORT; *forte* (Italian), adjective: loudly, as in music; pronounced FORtay

forthcoming, forthright

forthcoming: coming forth, about to appear, available or ready when needed.

forthright: frank, candid, direct, or straightforward.

gibe, jibe

gibe: jeer or taunt

jibe: to be in harmony, agreement, or accord; to shift from one side of a ship to the other

home, hone

home: to focus on or pinpoint (the missile homed in on the target)

hone: to sharpen

imminent, eminent

imminent: likely to happen soon

eminent: respected, prominent

immure, inure

immure: to confine, entomb, seclude, imprison

inure: get used to, habituate

infer, imply

infer: deduce, conclude

imply: suggest

innervate, enervate

innervate: to stimulate an organ or muscle

enervate: to exhaust or weaken

insure, ensure

insure: to provide insurance

ensure: to make safe or sure, to guarantee

irrelevant, irreverent

irrelevant: doesn't apply, beside the point

irreverent: disrespectful

lead, led

lead, noun: heavy grayish metal

led: past tense of the verb *lead*

loath, loathe

loath, adjective: reluctant (TH is pronounced like the TH in "moth.")

loathe, verb: despise (TH is pronounced like the TH in "other.")

luxurious, luxuriant

luxurious: lavish, opulent

luxuriant: healthy, growing, fertile, as a garden or plants

Milquetoast, milk toast

Milquetoast: meek or timid person

milk toast: buttered toast in hot milk

moral, morale

moral, noun: message, lesson, maxim; adjective: ethical, honorable, decent

morale: confidence, spirit, self-esteem

naval, navel

naval: pertaining to a navy

navel: place on the abdomen where the umbilical cord was attached, "bellybutton"

oral, aural

oral: pertaining to the mouth or speech

aural: pertaining to the ears or sound

ordinance, ordnance

ordinance: a law, rule, or decree

ordnance: military artillery, weapons, supplies

paean, peon

paean: a hymn giving thanks; a song of praise, triumph, joy

peon: servant

peak, peek, pique, piqué

peak: highest point

peek: steal a look, glance

pique, noun: anger, annoyance; verb: provoke or stimulate (pique one's interest)

piqué: a fabric

pedal, peddle

pedal: a lever or bar pressed by the foot

peddle: to sell

persecute, prosecute

persecute: to oppress, torment, punish

prosecute: to file suit against, bring to court, litigate, proceed to the end

phase, faze
phase: a stage in development
faze: disturb or trouble
phenomenon, phenomena
phenomenon: exceptional; any perceived process or occurrence
phenomena: plural of phenomenon
perspective, prospective
perspective: viewpoint; in art, perception of distance or dimension
prospective: future, expected (prospective buyer)
plumb, plum
plumb, adjective: to get to the bottom of (plumb the depths); noun:
 a device to measure or mark (as in depth, straightness, etc.);
 colloquial: completely (he was plumb bad from the start)
plum: a fruit
pore, pour
pore, verb: study or examine (he pored over the documents);
 noun: a small opening, as in skin
pour: cause to flow; issue, gush
postulate, postulant
postulate: hypothesize, propose, claim
postulant: candidate for a religious order
prerequisite, perquisite
prerequisite: requirement, precondition
perquisite: benefit beyond one's salary, "perk"
prescribe, proscribe
prescribe: to order, direct, mandate
proscribe: to prohibit
principal, principle
principal, noun: main or lead person; main part of a loan (as
 opposed to interest) or estate; adjective: main or most important (his principal goal is to entertain)
principle: canon, rule, controlling idea, ideal
prostrate, prostate
prostrate: flat on the ground, collapsed
prostate: a gland in men

ravage, ravish

ravage: to plunder, destroy

ravish: to rape; to charm, captivate, enthrall

refute, rebut

Refute means to disprove with conclusive evidence. We can *rebut* (dispute, deny, reject, challenge, contradict) a statement or argument, but that doesn't mean we've successfully *refuted* it.

retch, wretch

retch: to gag or vomit

wretch: a miserable or despised creature

sensual, sensuous

sensual: erotic, lustful

sensuous: providing beauty or pleasure through the senses

stationary, stationery

stationary: still, immobile

stationery: writing materials

taut, taunt

taut: stretched tight

taunt: to insult, jeer, ridicule

tic, tick

tic: spasm

tick: the sound of a clock; a check mark; bloodsucking bug

trooper, trouper

trooper: policeman, infantryman

trouper: actor, performer, team player

trustee, trusty

trustee: an executor; one administering a trust; board member who helps manage an institution, church, or business

trusty: a reliable and trusted person, often a prison inmate with special privileges and responsibilities

venerable, vulnerable

venerable: respected, revered

vulnerable: defenseless, exposed

want, wont

want: desire

wont, adjective: accustomed (as he is wont to do); noun: custom (that is his wont)

wangle, wrangle

wangle: to finagle, gain through trickery

wrangle: to quarrel, bicker; to herd livestock

wrack, rack

wrack: to twist, warp, contort, wrench

rack, noun: shelf or framework to hold things, a device for torture;

verb: to cause pain, to strain (racked his brain), collect or store (rack up points)

wreak, reek

wreak: to cause, bring about, perpetrate

reek: smell bad

yoke, yolk

yoke, noun: wooden frame resting on the shoulders or joining draft animals; servitude, burden, or bondage; verb: to fasten, couple, join

yolk: yellow center of an egg

CHAPTER 6

A Dozen Guidelines to Good Writing

Avoid Beginning With Long Dependent Phrases

Above all, I have tried to remove weight from the structure of stories and from language.

—Italo Calvino

Let's say you have an interesting morning. You have a long and harrowing commute to the office through a thunderstorm, and when you pull into your parking space, nerves frazzled, you're met by a masked man holding a gun.

"Gimme your dough and be quick about it," he barks hoarsely. Of course, you comply. Then you dash into the office and cry: "Someone just mugged me!" Or do you? Maybe you say instead: "Following a long and hazardous drive to the office through the rain this morning . . . ."

Or little Johnnie, who has been playing with Billy, runs up in tears. "Hey, what's the matter?" you ask, and he responds: "Billy hit me." Or maybe not. Maybe he says: "During an altercation in the sandbox . . . ."

Ridiculous, isn't it? But it shows how unnatural a habitual writing practice is—that of "backing into" an opening sentence with a long subordinate clause or phrase. We see this practice everywhere *except* in conversational writing—which should tell us what's wrong with it. We just don't talk that way. It isn't interesting or natural, and it violates one of the cardinal rules of good communication, whether in speech or writing—that of getting to the point.

We back into a sentence when we begin it with a preposition, verb, verbal, or with certain conjunctions and adverbs. Such a sentence is easy to recognize: It begins with a dependent phrase rather than with the sentence's *subject*, thereby delaying the subject and failing to make a clear point immediately. Here's an example from a book review:

> *Set firmly and with a sustained and vivid sensuous immediacy in the 19th century, and taking place mostly in the exotic world of the British West Indies though some scenes are set in London and the English countryside, the book tells two stories that are closely related, indeed inextricably joined in time and place.*

If this sentence were cast in subject-verb-object order, it might read: "The book, set largely in 19th century British West Indies, tells two closely related stories." Why are we omitting all that other stuff? Because, while it may *sound* good, it isn't logical. The book does not have a *firm* setting if it wanders all over for, what, a century. And writing that the book's action is both "sustained" *and* "immediate" is to choose words that fight with each other.

Why didn't this flawed opening sentence catch the editor's attention? That it did not shows us something important about backing-in phrases—people don't read them. The practiced eye skips the long dependent structure and flies ahead to the subject—that's where the solid information is.

> *Apparently trying to counter the notion of policy paralysis in the White House and a war campaign suddenly set adrift, the president . . . .*

Although the airline industry's attention right now is riveted on simplifying fares, filling up seats and ratcheting up profits, some executives . . . .

Because of a clash with the secretive Bachmann brothers over financial disclosure, Harold W. Simpson . . . .

These examples show why backing in is so uninviting—specially with the opening paragraph. We might occasionally and deliberately back into a sentence later in the piece for transition and variety in sentence structure. That's sensible as long as the resulting sentence is clear. Starting with a long and busy phrase is seldom attractive, however, because it violates clear and natural structure—subject, verb, and object, in that order. That's the way we generally think and speak in English: *actor — action — acted upon.*

You would not approach someone and say: *Apparently trying to counter the notion of policy paralysis in the White House and a war campaign suddenly set adrift . . . .* You wouldn't say that because, first, people would stop listening. And, second, you try not to bore and bewilder. The same applies to writing.

Happily, backed-into beginnings are easy to fix. We simply start with the subject. In the examples above, that's *the book, the president, executives,* and *Harold W. Simpson.* (Who's he, anyway? Withholding the subject is especially hazardous if the readers don't recognize him when he finally *does* show up.) If the material in the phrase is important, we can put it in the middle or at the end of the opening sentence—if it's short enough. If it is not, we can put that corollary idea in another sentence, but still in the opening paragraph.

The last sentence in the passage below shows the worst kind of backing in. Its opening phrase has 39 rudderless words, which readers must plow through before finding out that the sentence forms a transition from the word "inspiration" in the first sentence:

*Richard Condon says he doesn't often leave his unpreten-
tious home—and doesn't need to—for inspiration. 'All you have
to do is read The New York Times. They tell it like it ain't many
times,' he says. With a living room table strewn with copies
of Gourmet, The New Yorker, Mother Jones, The Washington
Monthly, American Film, Common Cause and The Nation, and
shelves loaded with books about wine, the CIA, transportation,
Nazi Germany, and England, the best-selling author apparently
finds other sources of inspiration as well.*

If it's risky to begin with a phrase, it's even more hazardous
to begin with a structure containing a long, unanchored list.
The solution is easy: Scratch that "list" structure, and place it
after the subject, "the best-selling author." That keeps the two
inspirations close together, making their relationship clear.

*Richard Condon says he doesn't often leave his unpreten-
tious home—and doesn't need to—for inspiration. 'All you
have to do is read The New York Times. They tell it like it
ain't many times,' he says. The best-selling author apparently
finds other sources of inspiration as well. His living room table
is strewn with copies of Gourmet, The New Yorker, Mother
Jones, The Washington Monthly, American Film, Common
Cause and The Nation . . . .*

We see that the worst fault of backing-in sentences is that
they hide the subject. Readers learn some corollary thing about
the subject before they even know what that subject is. So we
have some disembodied action, but nobody performing it. Or
we have background or explanation before we know what or
whom we're talking about. The longer and busier the phrase,
the fuzzier and more forbidding the approach:

*Armed with a structural evaluation report from the
Adamsville engineering firm of Chalmer Stevens Hennings &
Scott, ready to ask the city council for $2 million to renovate the*

dock, backed by members of the Early Days Antique Carousel Society and preservationists who adore old buildings, Michael Flaherty stands as the dock's last savior.

Again, imagine saying that to someone. Wouldn't it be nice if that passage began: "Michael Flaherty may finally be the dock's savior. Others have tried and failed, and Flaherty won't try it alone. He's armed with . . . ."

Numbers and statistics are naturally dense and forbidding— who opens a letter from the IRS or an annual report *eagerly?* Coupling numbers with a backed-into beginning assures that the work will find few readers:

As exports from both Western Europe and the third world—which had grown for the first five months of the year—fell in June and imports from both spheres rose, the U.S. trade deficit widened massively in June to $12.1 billion, the largest increase since February 1988. This was especially true of trade with Western Europe. The deficit with Japan also rose, and the value of the U.S. dollar plummeted toward a new post-World War II level against the Japanese yen before the Federal Reserve intervened to support the dollar in the currency markets and shored up its value against the yen.

Again, starting with the subject rather than the action clarifies the writing:

The U.S. trade deficit grew in June to $12.1 billion, the largest increase since February 1988. Falling exports and rising imports—especially in trade with Western Europe— caused the shortfall.

The deficit with Japan also rose and sent the dollar tumbling briefly against the yen. The Feds quickly restored its value, however, by buying huge amounts of U.S. money in foreign exchange markets.

Withholding the subject offers an added risk—as I suggested earlier regarding the "Harold Simpson" passage—when the "payoff" for the buildup is someone or something unknown:

> *As officials handed Indonesian computer expert Jarianto Hijawa the country's first "green card" on Monday, many expressed concern that anti-foreigner attacks would undermine the initiative by discouraging highly trained workers from moving to Germany.*

That lead displays the usual weaknesses of backing in. The phrase delays the main point while obscuring the real point. Since the readers never heard of Jarianto Hijawa, his presence at the story's opening is more bewildering than it is interesting. And the phrasing "as officials handed . . . many expressed concern" is a weak attempt to produce drama from flat and hackneyed expression.

With a little thought, we can clarify and streamline the main point and hold Jarianto Hijawa for the second paragraph, where we can make something of his presence.

> *Germany began its green card program for highly trained foreigners Monday, but officials said they feared that hostility toward foreigners might hinder the effort to attract expert workers to the country.*
>
> *An Indonesian, Jarianto Hijawa, received the nation's first green card. A computer expert, Hijawa . . . .*

Is there no such thing as an effective backed-into beginning? Yes, to be sure. Here's a purposeful one from David O'Reilly of *The Philadelphia Inquirer*. It begins a story on author Jack Miles and his book *God: A Biography*, which won the Pulitzer Prize:

> *Quick to anger yet profoundly just, at times uncertain yet all-knowing, pitying yet inexplicably bloodthirsty, he stands like a god in Western consciousness.*
>
> *That's because he is God.*

O'Reilly has a reason to withhold the subject—that subject is the punch line. Here's another effective backed-into beginning, from Jerry Siegel and Joe Shuster, the creators of Superman:

Faster than a speeding bullet, more powerful than a loco-motive, able to leap tall buildings at a single bound—look, up there in the sky, it's a bird, it's a plane, it's Superman!

As I say repeatedly throughout this book, the best way to engage the audience's attention, whether in speech or prose, is to get right to the point. And the best way to get right to the point is to give the reader a subject, then a verb, then an object. That structure is called the active or emphatic voice for a good reason: That's what it is. And no clear, compelling writer would consent to be less than active and emphatic.

Again, backing in can bring variety to the story's body. More rarely, it can work even in the opening sentence. A short backing-in phrase isn't going to hurt anything: "Last year in Chicago," "During the Roosevelt administration," "When I was a child." The dangerous and forbidding structure is the long one with disembodied action, but no subject to perform it. We should back in only when:

1) we've considered the alternatives.

2) we know what we're doing and why.

3) we have specific stylistic purposes that the backing-in structure satisfies.

CHAPTER 7

A Dozen Guidelines to Good Writing

Prefer Active Verbs and the Active Voice

The artist must imitate that which is . . . active, through form and figure.

—Samuel Coleridge

Here's an item from a city government instruction manual: *Instead of accepting charges indiscriminately and giving them docket numbers, complainants are counseled immediately.*

Does that passage seem an instruction or an observation? It seems an observation, which tells us in part what is often wrong with the passive voice—it's unclear. "Are counseled" is a passive construction: *Who* does the counseling? The *actor* is missing. The actor in instructions (*you*) is understood and, therefore, most instructions begin with a verb: (You) Do this; (You) Do that. Making that instruction manual passage active clarifies its intent and makes it sound like an instruction: *Counsel complainants immediately instead of routinely accepting charges and assigning docket numbers.*

Getting in the habit of using active verbs will keep you from dealing in unnecessary or unattractive passive constructions. Notice I said *unnecessary or unattractive.* Sometimes writing gurus exhort: *Avoid the passive voice!* We'll have none of that here. The passive voice has its reasons, and it's not only OK but preferable to use it in some cases.

In case you're rusty, the passive voice shakes up the normal subject-verb-object order—the acted-upon is in the *actor* position, and the actor is in the *acted-upon* position (if it's there at all):

Active: *The boy hit the ball.*
Passive: *The ball was hit by the boy.*
Passive: *The ball was hit.*

That example shows why the passive construction is often deemed weak and flabby—and that it provides less information when it withholds the actor, as in "The ball was hit." The passive voice is widely misunderstood, although I don't know why it should be. Some think a sentence is in passive voice whenever it has an auxiliary verb or a "be" verb. Not so. It is true that the passive voice does include auxiliary verbs, but that doesn't mean that all sentences with auxiliary verbs are passive. "She *was walking* down the street" is active. So is "The authorities *have been looking* into the case."

Grammar checker software adds to the confusion. Those programs hunt for auxiliary verbs and when they find one, they warn: *This sentence may be passive.* In many cases, the sentence is not passive—it merely contains some form of the verb "to be" (*is, are, was, were, be, been, being,* or *am*) as an auxiliary.

Here are more examples of passive and active sentences:

Active: *Students must declare their majors before the third semester.*
Passive: *A major course of study must be declared by the students before the third semester.*
Passive: *A major course of study must be declared before the third semester.*
Active: *The president announced my promotion.*
Passive: *My promotion was announced by the president.*
Passive: *My promotion was announced.*

Active: *The tour bus picked up the visitors.*
Passive: *The visitors were picked up by the tour bus.*
Passive: *The visitors were picked up.*

Each of those passive constructions is weak, long, or withholds vital information. When might the passive voice be more effective than the active? When the *actor* is irrelevant or gets in the way of the main point: *Doe's novel was acknowledged a masterpiece at the outset.* Who acknowledged that? Who cares? The emphasis here is on the artistry of the work, not on those who recognized its artistry. Straining to make the passive construction active would actually distort the statement's intent: *Lots of people acknowledge that Doe's novel was a masterpiece at the outset.* This version, although active, wrongly focuses on "lots of people." Here are further examples of effective passive constructions:

The company's mission statement has been completed.
The absentee policy has been found effective.
The package was delivered to the wrong address.

Again, *who* completed the mission statement, or found the policy effective, or delivered the package is irrelevant to the sense of those statements.

Writing with active verbs isn't always a subject-verb-object matter. Sometimes it simply means substituting a single active verb for a handful of weaker words. For example:

Marie Andrews *was dominant in* the event's bicycle phase.

Marie Andrews *dominated* the event's bicycle phase.

Single, strong verbs invigorate expression. *Decided* is stronger than "made a decision." *Substituted, intended, tried,* or *demonstrated* is stronger than "made a substitution," "have the intention," "made an effort," or "gave a demonstration."

Here's a simple quiz. Change flabby or repetitive phrasing to a single active verb.

1. We managed to determine the project's deadline.
2. The president has made a request that employees give their support to community arts.
3. The group offered a donation of food and clothing to the charity.
4. Please provide us with a summary of your proposal.
5. This equipment will serve to make reductions in maintenance cost over time.
6. We want to make progress toward the goal of better communication skills.
7. Please do a study of the policy's effects.
8. Take the corner of the paper and make a fold on the dotted line.
9. Give them an estimate of your total cost after you've done a calculation of the new figures.
10. You will please note that Ms. Ames made an objection.

Active verb revisions:
1. We determined the project's deadline.
2. The president asked employees to support community arts.
3. The group donated food and clothing to the charity.
4. Please summarize your proposal.
5. This equipment will reduce maintenance cost over time.
6. Our goal is better communication skills.
7. Please study the policy's effects.
8. Fold the paper on the dotted line.
9. Estimate your total cost after you've calculated the new figures.
10. Please note that Ms. Ames objected.

Whether you flip the sentence around to get your actor in the right place or compress several words into one strong verb, you'll find that your writing will be clearer and more vigorous for the effort. Oh, and by the way: shorter!

CHAPTER 8

A Dozen Guidelines to Good Writing

Cut Wordiness

They answered everything they could,
And wrote with all their might,
But though they wrote it all by rote,
They did not write it right.

—Arthur Clement Hilton

Everything we've discussed leads to this chapter. We've seen repeatedly that a chief secret of good writing is making every word count—wordiness is the main enemy of a clear, brief, and purposeful writing style. The best writers, whether of fiction or nonfiction, insist that every word carry its own load of meaning.

We've also seen how a conversational style contributes to good writing. As valuable as conversational writing is, however, it has a downside: It's likely to be wordy. Speech itself is notoriously wordy, but one important difference between speech and writing is that writing offers the luxury of editing. We can't effectively edit ourselves as we speak. We must plunge ahead even when we realize we're fashioning a long or awkward sentence—listeners won't wait while we edit orally: *hem, haw,* back up, and start over.

The potential for wordiness notwithstanding, it's best to write quickly and conversationally. When you finish, your first job will be to "blow off the chaff." That kind of editing is often easy—you have only to recognize wordiness and redundancies.

Certain words and structures point to windy writing. Prepositions, for example, often accompany wordiness, so cutting prepositional phrases (the subject of Chapter 10) has a corollary benefit of tightening the writing. This is particularly true when one word can substitute for a whole phrase. For example:

> **in** regard **to**: *about*
> **in** the event that: *if*
> a sufficient number **of**: *enough*
> **in** the vicinity **of**: *near*
> were **in** agreement: *agreed*
> **on** a daily basis: *daily*
> were **in** attendance: *attended*
> **on** the occasion that: *when*
> **at** this point **in** time: *now*
> are **of** the belief: *believe*

Unnecessary repetition, redundancies, and near redundancies also contribute to wordiness. For example: basic fundamentals (*fundamentals*); consensus of opinion (*consensus*); potential promise (*potential*); past history (*history*); personal friendship (*friendship*); total effect (*effect*); end result (*result*).

It and *there* sentence beginnings are often wordy. Consider this novelist's description of a garden:

> **There was**, indeed, plenty to see even in the fading light of an autumn day . . . .**There was** a small lawn surrounding a fish pond and edged with crazy paving. **There was** a succession of trellis archways leading from one carefully tended plot to another. **There was** a rose garden with a sundial where a few last roses still gleamed white on their leafless stems. **There were** hedges of beech, yew and hawthorn as gold and green backcloths to the banked chrysanthemums.

That passage is more active and purposeful without idle *there* constructions:

> *The garden presented a rich vista even in the fading light of an autumn day . . . . Trellis archways separated the carefully tended plots, and a small lawn edged with crazy paving surrounded a fish pond. A sundial stood at the heart of a rose garden, where a few last blooms gleamed white on leafless stems. Hedges of beech, yew, and hawthorn formed gold and green backcloths to the banked chrysanthemums.*

Imprecise or unnecessary adverbs and qualifiers also can lead to wordiness: "moved quickly" instead of *rushed* or *hurried*. Vagueness can cause wordiness; so, paradoxically, can unnecessary specificity:

> *Educators from many of the country's top high schools and most selective higher-education institutions meeting at a Harvard conference are discussing what many described as one of the greatest barriers to educational change: the high schools' own success.*

Phrasing such as "many," "most," "meeting at a conference," "what many described as" is only *seeming* specificity. In fact, it does nothing but add chaff to an otherwise brief and meaningful statement: *Educators at a Harvard conference on high schools are pondering one of the greatest barriers to educational reform: successful schools.*

Specifying the obvious also contributes to wordiness: "Jim Little spent the past 10 years quietly working behind the scenes to develop a computer system that would provide the public and the media with election results as quickly as possible." *The past 10 years*: Of course those years are past. *Quietly* and *behind the scenes* are near redundancies as well as off the point—Little's effort was in no way clandestine or secret. *Provide the public and the media*: provide, period. *As quickly as possible*: immediately. Improved: "Jim Little spent a decade developing a computer system that would provide immediate election results."

Pointless verb strings and unnecessary passives contribute to wordiness: "They need to start talking about" is better phrased: *they should discuss.* "The estimates will be submitted by the contractors next week" is tighter without the passive "by": *The contractors will submit estimates next week.* Choosing noun-heavy phrasing also causes verbiage: "give consideration to" should be *consider;* "have the need for" should be *need.*

As we saw in the last chapter, using a handful of words instead of one active verb also leads to wordiness. "Sixth-grader Molly Coddle was declared the winner in Davis County's student spelling bee." Change "was declared the winner in" to "won": "Sixth-grader Molly Coddle won Davis County's student spelling bee."

Whatever the cause of windy writing, the result is the same: loose, lazy, meandering prose.

Here are sentences that round up some of the usual wordiness suspects. Try to spot the problems and recast the sentence. Suggested revisions follow.

1. They are of the opinion that the agency needs to make changes in its proposal.

2. Prior to moving to Chicago, he lived in the city of Philadelphia.

3. She enrolled in this class in view of the fact that philosophy is a subject in which she takes an interest.

4. The fact that you didn't seek our advice subsequent to the meeting makes us feel disappointment.

5. There were three or four people on the committee who said that the companies who were bidding needed to give a demonstration of how the new equipment functions.

6. Some residents of the suburb of Oakwood have a tendency to consider the neighborhood a bedroom community.

7. There were 108 accidents in the targeted area during the crackdown, down from 145 during the same time period last year.

8. Military officers need to have knowledge and an understanding of their troops.

9. As per our telephone conversation, enclosed please find information on a new blocking device that prevents computer hackers from gaining access to your computer equipment and records.

10. The true facts of the matter are that the university has set a new record this year in receipt of free gifts and cash donations.

Revisions:

1. They think the agency should change its proposal.

2. He lived in Philadelphia before moving to Chicago.

3. She took this class because philosophy interests her.

4. We're disappointed that you didn't seek our advice after the meeting.

5. Several committee members said the bidding companies should demonstrate the new equipment.

6. Some Oakwood residents consider it a bedroom community.

7. During the crackdown, the number of accidents in the targeted area fell to 108, down from 145 last year.

8. Military officers should know and understand their troops.

9. Here's information on a blocking device that can keep hackers out of your computer system.

10. The university has received record gift and cash donations this year.

CHAPTER 9

Avoid Vague Qualifiers

One of our defects as a nation is a tendency to use what have been called 'weasel words.' When a weasel sucks eggs the meat is sucked out of the egg.

—Theodore Roosevelt

I can't be the only one who'd be pleased never again to hear or see the word *very*. It's the most rampant four-letter word in English—yes, even considering other rampant four-letter words. *Very* drains life and vigor from otherwise robust expression. Intended to heighten, it merely flattens.

Listen to this educator: *We're trying very, very hard to improve our students' basic language skills, which are admittedly very low. It has been very challenging indeed, but we are very pleased to report some very small improvement after months of very intense effort.*

You think I'm exaggerating!

Her statement would be stronger and clearer without that simpering, say-nothing stinker *very*: "We're trying hard to improve our students' admittedly low language skills. It has been challenging, but we're pleased to report some improvement after months of intense effort."

Although such words as *very* are more excusable in speech than in print, we should curtail their use even there. The reason *very* and its siblings—*extremely, totally, completely, wholly, entirely, utterly, really, quite, rather, somewhat, slightly, fairly,* etc.—are useful in speech is that they help us get closer to our meaning when we can't think of the perfect word. If we can't instantly call to mind the right word, we fortify the less-than-right word with an intensifier such as *very, extremely, totally, wholly, entirely, utterly, really,* or *completely.* Or we tame it with *quite, rather, slightly, fairly,* or *somewhat.*

Writing, however, lets us review, reconsider, and revise. We can find the right word for our context and let it stand alone—rather than the almost right word, qualified.

Sometimes, dependence upon vague qualifiers is not purposeful but just a habit. The qualifiers aren't buttressing weak words or curbing strong ones—they're just *there.* The words they modify are perfectly fine standing alone. In such cases, qualifiers are chaff and should be blown off. Stripping gratuitous qualifiers creates a curious and welcome effect: The word left standing becomes stronger and more assertive in its solitude. Unnecessary qualifiers deplete instead of augment.

Read the following sentences aloud, and see how deleting the qualifiers streamlines, strengthens, and purifies.

Original: *When he was alone with her in the darkness on the seashore, he was very happy.*

Revised: When he was alone with her in the darkness on the seashore, he was happy.

Original: *It was a very ugly house, surrounded by a wild untended garden full of old fruit trees whose leaves lay in drifts on the grass. Its windows were the sash kind and very small, but its front door was enormous, quite out of proportion.*

Revised: It was an ugly house, surrounded by a wild untended garden full of old fruit trees whose leaves lay in drifts on the grass. Its windows were tiny, its enormous front door out of proportion.

Original: *Although they remembered the playwright as very austere, she found he had a somewhat playful, even rather mischievous, side.*

Revised: They remembered the playwright as austere, but she found him playful, even mischievous.

The vague qualifiers in those examples are chaff, a habit of conversation—*um, ah, ahem!* They add nothing. *Happy,* for example, is a strong, clear word, but if it's not enough, *overjoyed, thrilled,* or *ecstatic* has a precision that "very happy" lacks. The second example forces us to know the difference between the writer's conception of "ugly"—a sturdy, stand-alone word—and "*very* ugly." If it's *very* ugly, maybe it's *hideous*? From the description, we guess not; it's probably just ugly. And if *small* must be modified, can we find a more precise word—*tiny, minuscule, insignificant*? Likewise, *quite* only detracts from "out of proportion." Finally, why qualify *austere, mischievous, playful*? Those words aren't lame and don't need crutches.

Some words are so independent that qualifying them is not just unnecessary, but wrong. You can't sensibly modify words that have no degrees of meaning. Can we properly say "*slightly* dead," for example, or "*somewhat* alive"? "*Rather* unique" is as ridiculous as "rather pregnant" or "rather malignant." And such structures as "*completely* destroyed" and "*totally* demolished" are redundant.

Sometimes intensifiers such as *very* are simply inflationary—a way of exclaiming instead of explaining:

Original: *The funds for the multilingual program are necessary given how very diverse the district is.*

Better: Funding the multilingual program is necessary given the district's diversity.

Best: Funding the multilingual program is necessary because the district's students speak more than a dozen languages.

The final revision is best because it scraps that weary word *diversity*, adds vital and concrete information, and explains rather than exclaims.

As we see from the above examples, a good test for whether we have the right word is whether it can stand alone. If we describe something as *rather* beautiful, then that something is probably less than beautiful. Maybe it's just *attractive*. If we describe something as *very* beautiful, then it's probably beyond beautiful—maybe it's *exquisite*.

It's a shame to sacrifice English's huge lexicon of more than 600,000 words—words rich in degree of meaning. If our work is littered with qualifiers whose only function is, as Shakespeare wrote, "to gild refined gold, to paint the lily," we should kick the qualifier habit. Very soon—as in very, very soon. As in immediately.

CHAPTER 10

Prune Prepositions

What is written without effort is in general read without pleasure.

—Samuel Johnson

We hear much about the role nouns and verbs play in good writing but little about the role prepositions play in *poor* writing. Consider:

> Donald Davis, one **of** three law enforcement officers acquitted **in** the drowning deaths **of** three youths **in** Harrisburg stood **by** his pickup Monday **at** his home **by** the railroad tracks **in** Smithville and slowly, **in** a voice void **of** emotion said, 'It feels good.' That morning, he had dressed **in** a shirt, tie, and slacks and returned **to** his old desk **in** the probation department **on** the third floor **of** the Mitchell County courthouse.

Prepositions are vital, of course. What would we do without *in, of, by, for, on,* and so forth? But as useful as those compact little words are, they must be limited and controlled or they'll fill the sentence with chaff, disrupt its flow, and force its rhythms into an annoying singsong.

Controlled prepositions, however, can be more than just useful. Take the deliberate repetition *of the people, by the people, for the people.* It capitalizes on what such phrases can bring: parallel structure, scripted pauses, predictable rhythm. Notice, though, that both emphasis and beauty come from the repeated word *people* rather than from the prepositions. *Of the people, by the electorate, for the masses* is hardly pleasing. It merely destroys the original's deliberate harmony.

Of the people, by the people, for the people illustrates the "rule of three"—which, in the case of prepositions, is hardly a rule. But it is a useful generalization and guideline. A sentence generally can bear three prepositional phrases, but it breaks down rapidly if more are added after that—and the more prepositions added, the worse the breakdown.

Special effects aside, we'll write clearer, cleaner, and more energetic sentences if we fill them with nouns, verbs, and adverbs rather than with prepositions and prepositional phrases. Also, some prepositional phrases can be rendered adjective-plus-noun: "The members of the faculty" can be "faculty members," for example, or "the door of the car" can be "car door."

Consider: "Crime is increasing *at an explosive rate.*" That would be better without the prepositional phrase "at an explosive rate" and with, for example, the verb *exploding*: "The crime rate is exploding." Or we could choose the adverb *explosively*: "Crime is rising explosively."

Another example: "*In* general, the people want to be assured that the issue *of* the economy *of* the nation is being dealt *with in* a professional manner *by* the government." We can rewrite that: "The people want assurance that the government is handling the nation's economy with care." Or even better because it's more conversational: "The people want to know that the nation's economy is in good hands."

Those revisions are stronger not only because they lose prepositions, but also because they lose unnecessary "to be" and passive voice structures. The revisions are also tighter. Pruning prepositions often brings such unexpected dividends.

We can generally lose prepositions without losing information: *"After* lunch, we float *down* the river, watching a gaggle *of* harbor seals play an aquatic version *of* hide and seek and take *in* a performance *of* bald eagles *as* they spiral and soar *on* thermal updrafts above."* To reduce the number of prepositions and lose no information: "After lunch, we floated downstream, where harbor seals played aquatic hide-and-seek and bald eagles soared on thermal updrafts."

Another example: "Success *in* the past was generated *by* combining outstanding automotive design *with* state-of-the-art manufacturing methodology *at* production facilities located *throughout* the country. The product was then sold *through* an international network recognized as one *without* peer."

Revision: "We've been successful because we combined outstanding automotive design with the latest manufacturing methods and sold our product through a peerless international network."

If trimming prepositions sacrifices incidental information, it can easily be placed in subsequent sentences. Readability is more important than squeezing in every scrap of information:

Original: "*In* the presidential election, voters living *in* the five localities *of* the district cast 72 percent *of* their ballots *for* Al Gore."

Revised: "In the presidential election, 72 percent of the district voted for Al Gore." (The corollary information that the district has five localities can be placed elsewhere; it isn't necessary to the sentence.)

Original: "Many members *of* the faculty wanted to take advantage *of* this opportunity to expand the incentive to remediate students *in* science and social studies. The remediation and recovery program is *of* great value *with* respect *to* English and math."

Revised: "The remedial program has been so successful in English and math that many faculty members wanted to expand it to science and social studies."

Even when excessive prepositional phrases don't damage clarity, they damage flow: "*In* the damp sand is a multitude *of* tracks—the hoof prints *of* a deer, the light trident markings left behind *by* a blue heron seeking fish and frogs. Each toe is clearly visible *in* a set *of* bear paw prints—as are the claws." The following revision not only cuts that passage's prepositions but also gains elegance and precision: "Tracks litter the damp sand: a deer's carved hoof print, a blue heron's faint trident marking, a bear paw imprint with clearly etched toe and claw."

Clarity is the most important issue, however:

> *There is increasing evidence that Enron's board, composed of many prominent and financially sophisticated people, was actively involved in crucial decisions that may have led to the company's downfall. While the board fired Andersen as Enron's auditor Thursday and contended it only learned of the serious concerns raised about the company's accounting and financial practices in October, the directors appear to have played a significant role in overseeing the partnerships at the center of Enron's collapse.*
>
> *The board—which includes Wendy L. Gramm, a former government regulator and the wife of Senator Phil Gramm, Republican of Texas; John Wakeham, a member of the British House of Lords and a former British cabinet leader; and Norman P. Blake Jr., the chief executive of Comdisco, a computer services company—even went so far as to suspend Enron's code of ethics to approve the creation of the partnership between Enron and its chief financial officer, according to the report of a preliminary study conducted at Enron's request by the law firm of Vinson & Elkins.*

There's more wrong with that passage than excessive prepositions, but *any* two sentences containing 24 prepositions would be unreadable, no matter what else might be going on.

The second sentence presents a board action as well as the implicit suggestion that the board includes people of prominence, sophistication, and impressive background. But the first sentence explicitly makes that very point. The only new information in the second sentence is Andersen's firing, corollary information that could as easily go into a third paragraph. A chief problem with the first sentence is its vague reference to Enron's partnerships as "at the center of Enron's collapse." Briefly explaining the effect of those partnerships would clarify that phrasing.

More challenging is the second sentence, a 96-word monstrosity so bad it simply stuns. It's not only too long but also poorly crafted. The 49-word interruption between actor (*the board*) and action (*went so far as*) is a list, and well-crafted lists are often exempt from sentence- length concerns—*if* they stand alone or are at sentence end. (See the discussion on lists in Chapter 1.) But this list intervenes between subject and verb, and the obvious happens. We get so entangled in the long and busy interruption that when we reach the verb, we no longer remember what it belongs to and must back up and re-read.

Beyond structural problems, we have those 24 prepositions. Here's a revision:

> *Growing evidence suggests that Enron's board of directors, which includes many prominent and financially adept members, made decisions contributing to the company's downfall. The law firm Vinson & Elkins, which Enron hired to study the company's accounting practices, says the board waived the company's ethics code to approve partnerships between the company and its chief financial officer. Those partnerships kept much of the company's debt off its books and masked its huge losses.*
>
> *Enron's board includes Wendy L. Gramm, a former government regulator and wife of Texas Republican Senator Phil Gramm; John Wakeham, member of the British House of Lords and former British cabinet leader; and Norman P. Blake Jr., chief executive of Comdisco, a computer services company.*

> *The board fired Andersen as Enron's auditor Thursday and contends that it first learned of concerns regarding the company's accounting and financial practices in October. The report's disclosures leave little doubt, however, that . . . .*

Obviously, we can't cut all prepositions, nor should we try. But keeping them to a minimum offers a quick route to clarity, simplicity, and brevity.

CHAPTER 11

Limit Number and Symbol

The great artist is the simplifier.

—Henri-Frederic Amiel

The "rule of three," which we discussed regarding prepositions, also applies to how many numbers a sentence can bear. A useful guideline is to limit to three the numbers in a sentence—three seems to be all the reader's brain can handle *if* those numbers require comparison, contrast, or calculation of some kind. Here's an all-too-typical sentence made unreadable by numbers.

> *The Dow Jones industrial average of 30 stocks rose as much as 52.02 to a new high of 4,816.9, surpassing a previous peak set September 13, before closing at 4,793.78, up 28.90, with the week's gain for the Dow being 24.57.*

What does that sentence need? A couple of periods. Short sentences are especially helpful in number-heavy passages, so careful writers cut up unmanageable slabs into bite-size pieces:

> *The Dow Jones industrial average rose as much as 52.02 during the day to a new high of 4,816.9, surpassing a previous*

peak set September 13. The Dow closed at 4,793.78, up 28.90. The week's gain for the Dow, which comprises 30 stocks, was 24.57.

Numbers are even more confusing when they have different forms—that is, percentages, fractions, written out, numerals, etc. Consider the following unreadable newspaper passage: "The 9th grade students did well on most of the 3-part test with at least 85 percent of the students at more than two-thirds of the schools passing seven of the 28 test objectives."

That sort of muddy writing maddens editors as well as readers. It's impossible to understand at first reading. Even taking the sentence apart and absorbing it a few words at a time fails to clarify, and editors probably would be reluctant to rewrite without the writer's being present to verify the work.

Also critical is the presence of symbols. A passage laden with numbers will be especially forbidding if it also contains other visually uninviting material—dollar signs, decimals, percentage symbols, acronyms, or abbreviations. The result can strike the reader's eye as alphabet soup: "NationsBank Corp., created by the merger of NCNB Corp. and CD&S-Sovran Corp., reported Monday it lost $244 million, or $1.08 per share, in the fourth quarter of 1991."

That sentence would be immensely improved in both appearance and content by holding for a later sentence "created by the merger of NCNB Corp. and CD&S-Sovran Corp." That would yield a clarified and visually more attractive "NationsBank Corp. reported Monday it lost $244 million, or $1.08 per share, in the fourth quarter of 1991."

Appearance is of special importance when dealing with numbers and symbols. Writers naturally tend to *write*, forgetting that prose and textual presentation is uninviting when dealing with certain kinds of material. Graphic explanation—bulleted lists, tabulated material, charts, white space—is as easy to execute as words and is both clearer and more attractive.

Even a relatively straightforward "number" paragraph benefits from a simple graphic presentation:

> *Student financial aid climbed 7.9 percent last year to a record $30.8 billion, with students receiving $15.1 billion in grants, $14.9 billion in loans, and $791 million in workstudy earnings.*

That passage is more inviting and easier to read and understand as:

Student aid climbed 7.9 percent last year to a record $30.8 billion. Students received:
- *$15.1 billion in grants*
- *$14.9 billion in loans*
- *$791 million in work-study earnings*

There are two common exceptions to this three-number guideline. The first exception is a sentence in which some numbers are *dates*. For example, a sentence might compare multiple figures for multiple years and be perfectly clear. That's because the numerals identifying *years* require no calculation or study. They don't create the same sort of "number clutter" as other numerals—they are like nouns (the "names" of the years) and are thus static. So you might have, say, a perfectly clear six-number sentence because three of the numbers are dates: *The dean said he expected enrollment to increase by 20 percent in 2004, 10 percent in 2005, and 15 percent in 2006.*

The second exception is a sentence in which more than three numbers run consecutively, but each has the same form and identifies the same thing—for example, yardages in a football story. The reader could handle, for example: "Johnson threw touchdowns of 6, 63, 78, and 26 yards, giving the Hawks the lead." But that sentence becomes unreadable when other numbers are added:

Johnson threw touchdowns of 6, 63, 78 and 26 yards, giving the Hawks, 2-1, a 41-38 lead with 1:52 to play, but with three seconds left in regulation, Tony Enrico kicked a 52-yard field goal for Smithville, his longest of the season, sending the game into overtime.

We see from the examples above that controlling numbers—both quantity and kind—is critical to clarity, whatever the subject.

CHAPTER 12

A Dozen Guidelines to Good Writing

Get Right to the Point. And Stay There.

One begins with two people on the stage, and one of them had better say something pretty damn quick.

—Moss Hart

When I was teaching creative writing to university students, the greatest challenge to most students was, first, getting to the point, and second, getting there *quickly*. At semester's beginning, they might write something like: "It startled him, and he gave her a quick look. Then he moved quickly to the door, turned the knob, pulled it open, and disappeared from the room."

If I challenged that passage as dithering and failing to get to the point, the student might say: *But I did get to the point—he left the room.* It seldom occurred to the student to write exactly that: *He left the room.* Or, to capture the whole passage: *He sent her a startled glance and left the room.*

Trivial action was a problem. Small actions such as getting someone out of a room became arduous pursuits. If we had been writing drama, we could have written: *Exit stage left.* But we were writing narrative, and our goal was to get the guy out of the room without making the readers roll their eyes. That means trusting the readers enough to know they will suppose the character turned the knob and left the room by a door—if it matters and if they care.

Below is the beginning of a story from a professional writer that would have benefited greatly from not only getting to the point, but also getting there quickly. Writers sometimes don't realize that an inherently dramatic tale is made even more dramatic through focus, purpose, compression, and underwriting. They often overwrite the dramatic story, which paradoxically drains it of its strength.

> *The door exploded with a noise that shattered the midnight sleep and Delie Grace struggled from the dark calm to see a man standing beside her bed waving a submachine gun.*
>
> *'What is your name? What is your name?' he shouted. 'Your name!'*
>
> *The shrieking voice came clipped out from under the balaclava helmet covering his head—the unmistakable hard tones of the Afrikaner.*
>
> *'Delie,' she said softly, shocked from subconsciousness.*
>
> *'Delie what?' said the crouched figure at the bedside.*
>
> *'Delie Grace,' she said, taking in the pattern of his camouflaged fatigues. It was South African.*
>
> *But what was a South African commando doing blasting his way into the second-story apartment of a widowed mother of three in the Swaziland capital of Mbabane in the middle of the night?*
>
> *For Grace, assistant to the head of a Unitarian Service Committee in Swaziland, the super-national political questions of southern Africa were, at that moment, a very simple matter.*
>
> *'Get up,' said the voice behind the mask.*
>
> *She did and was bundled out into her living room.*
>
> *'I called out to my children and when they didn't respond, I got very scared because I thought they had been killed,' she said.*

When a story is inherently dramatic, we make it even stronger by telling it simply and swiftly. A florid style or rhetorical devices such as repetition can seem melodramatic and may even seem to milk the subject. Worse, a melodramatic approach can seem ridiculous and thus may trivialize the tragic or poignant. Preserve drama and dignity by flying straight to the point, via speed, focus, and compression.

The point here, the pivotal paragraph, is this: "For Grace . . . the super-national political questions of southern Africa were, at that moment, a very simple matter." That's the point the writer wants to reach as quickly as possible. Revised:

> Delie Grace jerked awake from her midnight sleep and sat up in confusion. Her bedroom door had shattered in an explosion of sound, and a man waving a submachine gun stood at her bedside shrieking questions. He wore the mottled camouflage of South Africa, his clipped Afrikaner accent emerging from beneath a balaclava helmet and mask.
>
> 'Your name!' he screamed.
>
> 'Delie,' she whispered.
>
> 'Delie what?'
>
> 'Delie Grace.'
>
> 'Get up,' he ordered.
>
> At that moment, South African politics came down to one question for this widowed mother of three: Were her children killed?

That right-to-the-point approach underscores without milking or overselling fear and danger.

Anecdotes—as effective as they are when they work well—can blur the focus and delay getting to the point:

> Two flirtatious teenage Kuwaiti girls smile and wave at soldiers outside the U.S. Embassy from their cherry-red convertible. One is wearing skin-tight jeans, the other a short, hip-hugging skirt. Music blares from the car's speakers.

Draped across the back seat of the car are two abayas, the traditional black robes worn by Arab women and dictated by Islamic tradition, which dictates that women dress modestly.

Why are the abayas in the back seat?

'To get out of the house,' the driver of the convertible explains just as traffic begins to move.

Although Saudi Arabia, at least in public, is a bastion of strict Islamic virtues and values, Kuwaitis have always been decidedly more laid back. If Saudis are the Calvinists of Islam, Kuwaitis are its hedonists. They are the yuppies of the desert, conspicuous consumers par excellence. Pricey boutiques, shopping malls, and fast food restaurants abound.

The anecdotal beginning on this story about Kuwaiti lifestyle is brief but nonetheless dithering. Nor is it particularly interesting. Anecdotes can enliven an otherwise dry beginning, but the anecdote should be short and pertinent. It should reveal something important about the story's theme and thus open a way in to the story. More intriguing than the two girls, who seem pretty normal, is the Calvinist/hedonist analogy. The writer should focus tightly and go for the grist:

If Saudis are Islam's Calvinists, Kuwaitis are its hedonists. The laid-back Kuwaitis—with their pricey boutiques, shopping malls, and fast food restaurants—have never been big on austerity.

Think of them as the yuppies of the desert.

Anecdotes are just one way of delaying the point. Sometimes writers create questions in the reader's mind—which can be a useful device for provoking curiosity—but provide no answers.

The Smithville School District is about to embark on by far its boldest move in many years to make what goes on in thousands of classrooms more responsive to the needs of its more than 30,000 students, school officials said.

That beginning presents empty words rather than substance. What is the district going to do, exactly, and how will it affect children and their education, exactly? In short, what is the point?

Here's another example of offering the reader vacant verbiage instead of solid information:

> *State legislators are trying to break their deadlock on education reform and could pass a significant measure this session after all.*
>
> *The House Friday unanimously approved a compromise bill worked out the previous day in informal discussions between House Education Chairman John Fitzsimmons and his counterpart in the Senate, Peter Hudson. The bill would send state schools down the road educators have been advocating for years. It calls for less state meddling in local education decisions, but more clear and consistent standards to assure Washington the state is conforming to viable principles of excellence.*

If this story has a point, it's missing so far. Again, the approach frustrates readers because it creates unanswered questions. Legislators are breaking unspecified deadlocks, contemplating unidentified significant measures, approving an undefined compromise, and sending schools down some unnamed road. The point of the passage is what legislators are doing, and that's the very point the writer refuses to reveal.

The last two examples show the difference between creating in the readers a healthy sense of curiosity and frustrating them with unanswered questions. We'll discuss that subject further in chapters 15 and 16. For now, it's enough to observe that failure to get right to the point and stay there—whether from overwriting and wordiness, an ill-advised anecdote, or a dithering, vague style—is a chief cause of reader annoyance.

STORYTELLING DEVICES

CHAPTER 13

Storytelling: The Narrative Engine

Archetype, Character, and Plot

> *There are only two or three human stories, and they go on repeating themselves as fiercely as if they had never happened before.*
> —Willa Cather

The word *narrative* is sometimes spoken in hushed and bewildered tones—especially by media writers, whose immersion in the "inverted pyramid" can make storytelling a foreign notion. The word could hardly be easier to apprehend—it means *story*, plain and simple. To narrate is to tell, as with a story, or to provide a spoken commentary, as with film or television. The narrative is the story itself. And the narrative or story *line* is the thread upon which the "beads" of the story are strung.

Inverted pyramid or summary organization is a report-writing, not a storytelling, style. It organizes material in *descending* order of importance—not for interest, but for quick and easy transmittal of information. It's efficient for news and therefore appropriate for much informational and media writing.

Narrative, however, differs from reportorial writing in that it seeks to immediately create curiosity rather than to immediately satisfy it. The inverted pyramid—because it's a summary of result or consequence—gives away the end at once, while narratives usually begin on the low end of a rising curve of action that builds to climax and resolution (or *dénouement*).

The word *narrative* comes from a Latin root that means "to know." That derivation underlines the traditional respect for storytellers. Those who "have the story" not only pass on truth, or history, or culture, but also are assumed to know and understand it. And, in fact, the more writers know about storytelling and its elements, the better writers they will be in any genre.

The necessary ingredients of narrative writing are characters and conflict, and its chief organizing elements are chronology, point of view, and setting. Stripped to its most basic, a narrative involves a hero (or heroine) facing a difficulty that the hero either vanquishes or is vanquished by. The narrative form is of course the natural vehicle for fiction. But the term "true story" is not an oxymoron. Narrative is also suitable for factual writing when there are characters *and* conflict *and* an over-arching question that drives story and reader toward the conclusion. The basic question in narrative writing is *what happened? Will the hero or heroine live, die, win, lose?*

Stephen King relates in *On Writing* how he wrote *Carrie*. Two unrelated ideas had come to him: adolescent cruelty and telekinesis, and he thought he could put them together in a yarn for a magazine. So he worked on the story for a while but didn't like it and threw the work away. Later, he writes, his wife presented him with the discarded pages:

> *She'd spied them while emptying my wastebasket, had shaken the cigarette ashes off the crumpled balls of paper, smoothed them out, and sat down to read them. She wanted me to go on with it, she said. She wanted to know the rest of the story.*

In wanting to know "the rest of the story," she was asking the over-arching question: *What happened?* And that compelling question led to Stephen King's finishing *Carrie*, whose paperback rights alone sold for $400,000.

The secret of a good narrative is that it entices and grips the reader by regenerating in the readers' minds the same curiosity that first involved the writer. When you're working on a story, remember the question that generated your story; let it be a chief organizing and focusing principle. You might even jot down the question. In the laborious and time-consuming process of gathering information and writing, you could forget why you started the thing in the first place.

What is the question that drives the action and the reader forward in *The Wizard of Oz*? Will Dorothy get home? *Moby Dick*: Will Ahab get the white whale or will the white whale get him? The television hit of more than a decade ago, "Twin Peaks": Who killed Laura Palmer?

Murder, of course, offers the quintessential question— whodunnit?

What are the over-arching questions in Fyodor Dostoevsky's classic *Crime and Punishment*, considered by many the first modern "psychological" novel? The initial question: Will Raskolnikoff kill that old woman? Then: Will he cause himself to get caught through his own guilt and paranoia? Then the biggest question of all, posited by the novel as a whole: Which is the true punishment—being caught, or the fear of being caught?

Archetype

Archetypes, too, drive a story forward—not only by creating questions, but also by creating expectations. The world's greatest and most memorable stories from *Oedipus* to *Hamlet* to *Old Man and The Sea* have been archetypal. They involve universals—principles that hold up over centuries and that our ancestors recognized as readily as we.

The archetype is as complex as the narrative is simple. Archetypes and the constructs of myth have great impact on us both emotionally and intellectually, as psychologist Carl Jung clearly demonstrated when working to support his theory of the collective unconscious. Joseph Campbell also has done fascinating work on archetype and myth, as has J.G. Frazer, Maud

Bodkin, and Ernst Cassirer. The study of archetype, myth, and language offers a rich field of inquiry for writers who wish to better understand and harness the power of story.

Archetypes are in a sense unknowable and ineffable. They can be like the shadow on a wall of Plato's cave: We see the shadow, but not the "thing" that casts it. It's necessary to realize this because to misunderstand the archetype and its function is to risk making of it a mere stereotype or cookie-cutter.

Archetypes are never stereotypes. Whether archetypes of character, action, or theme, they are atavistic and universal products of that Jungian "collective unconscious." They are the story behind the story, and outside the setting. Sometimes a story in a particular period or culture comes along and sweeps people off their feet, and copycats get busy, supposing that the setting was the attraction. But, as I read somewhere, setting is the gift wrap; story is the gift.

For our purposes, we can define the archetype as a template, prototype, model, paradigm, or exemplar of an *abstract* idea—or of a character or scheme of action. We could also call the latter plotting, of course, but the point here is that archetypes offer recognizable arrangements of behavior and action in which certain elements are predictable, or at least expected. (If the expected does not occur—in event, reward, or punishment—the work may seem lacking in artistic unity, coherence, and integrity and can sorely surprise or disappoint the audience.)

Before we discuss specific archetypes of action, theme, and character, let's briefly consider the distinctions of three major story types: tragedy, pathos, and bathos. There are others, of course. (We're saying nothing, for example, about comedy.) But those three will suffice for this discussion.

Tragedy

Tragedy yields the greatest, most compelling, and most memorable stories. It teaches, awes, provokes thought, inspires fear and compassion, and saddens because it involves waste.

A heroic figure, larger than life, noble, promising, multidimensional, has a flaw, a "fatal flaw," that brings about his or her downfall. The flaw often involves some form of *hubris*, which is Greek for "wanton insolence," and causes the hero to transgress or ignore natural law, rule, more, or convention. The hero's flaw may be pride, ambition, greed, lust, jealousy, a desire for revenge, naiveté. Whatever, he or she fails to see consequence. The tragic hero is his own victim.

Real life "tragic hero" stories are likewise compelling and often excite a good deal of public attention. Consider former presidents Richard Nixon and Bill Clinton—one an ambitious and seasoned leader who could have been a great statesman, but whose paranoid suspicions caused him to violate the very laws he had sworn to protect; the other a bright, charismatic leader who wasted his great promise on tawdry sexual shenanigans.

Now consider actor Marlon Brando's anguished "I coulda been a contender!" in the '50s film "On the Waterfront." Was Brando's misfit character a *tragic* hero? No, he was *pathetic*—he was not his own victim but a victim of people who betrayed him. Nor was he multi-dimensional. He had one gift; he could box. Outside the ring, he had neither promise nor particular coping skills.

A chief difference between tragedy and pathos is that in the latter, the principals are not active agents in their own destiny. Tragedy is more deeply satisfying than pathos in part because tragedy suggests causality or free will. The popular saying "let me at least be the hero of my own life" expresses both the fear of being someone else's victim and the need for personal autonomy and control.

Pathos

Pathos, then, presents a victim who is helpless in the face of circumstances not of his or her own making. If the story concerns only that victim, it's often reduced to a depressing one-dimensional drama with no real conflict between good and evil. (Many-layered stories such as "On the Waterfront," where other characters and action lend dimension and meaning, are exceptions to this generalization.) Coincidence or acts of nature may play a part in pathetic drama, thereby heightening the audience's frustrating sense of helplessness. Pathos is sad and inspires pity, but is not very *interesting* because there is nothing to learn from it; the audience experiences mostly pity and futility. Saint and martyr stories often fall into this category. That's why such tales are often spectacular failures with the public—to the surprise of their creators, who never seem to learn that something *else* must be presented besides the merely saintly or the merely martyred.

Bathos

Bathos presents a victim in maudlin, sentimental, and melodramatic action. Often the wholly good are destroyed by the wholly bad. Think of the characters in silent films—for example, the villain stroking his mustache and chuckling malevolently. Such characters were one-dimensional representations rather than real people. Bathos presents gratuitous moralizing, but there is nothing to learn and no dimension. It was popular at the height (some would say *depth*) of Victoriana but is out of fashion and repellent to modern audiences. Bathos still exists in the melodramatic potboiler, but for the most part, modern readers don't want a story "milked" or moralized. They want it told with restraint, clarity, and artistry, and they want to make their own judgment and interpretation.

Archetypal tales, from fairy tales and Aesop's Fables to *Madame Bovary* and *The Sweet Smell of Success*, are in their essence moral or cautionary tales. In contemporary art, they are sophisticated and subtle extrapolations of universal patterns. They seek cause, consequence, reason, and order. So does humankind. Accident or chaos terrifies us because we can't control it. It's unpredictable and ungoverned by natural law. All bets are off—nothing we can *do* will guarantee our safety. Most human activity is in one way or another a search for guarantee, for a sense of autonomy and control. Our abiding interest and satisfaction in archetypal stories spring in part from that search: *I see that if I do A, B might happen—therefore I will do A.* Or: *Therefore, I'll refrain from doing A.*

True horror always suggests chaos and unpredictability—think of Alfred Hitchcock's film "Psycho," for example, or Stephen Spielberg's "Jaws." Better, let's go straight to Shakespearean tragedy, which has thrived for more than 400 years. At play's end, the stage is littered with principal characters, and the audience is left trying to figure out what each did to cause such mayhem. The drama ends when a knowledgeable survivor steps onstage to make some sense of it all and to offer rousing remarks about restoring order. The audience needs and welcomes that promise.

We prefer the tragic mode because of that promise of causality and ensuing order. How strong is our natural antipathy toward the chaos and "victimhood" of pathos? It makes us seek a reason for victimization—in a sense, blaming the victim. Such behavior is common: *If he hadn't gone to that bar after work, if she hadn't worn such suggestive clothing, if they hadn't befriended the wrong people, if she hadn't been involved in drugs, if he hadn't picked that day to go to the park, if they hadn't changed their flight arrangements . . . .* Those responses may seem callous or even silly, but they show a natural rejection of happenstance (against which we have no defense) and a desire for a reason, for cause. We've been reared on archetypal lessons since Oedipus and before: *Be warned! If you sleep with your mother, you will put out your eyes before the play is over.*

The primary realities of our existence reflect thematic archetypes: *birth, coming of age, struggle, maturation, death.* Some other obvious theme or action archetypes are *quest, search, journey, pursuit, capture, rescue, escape, love, forbidden love, unrequited love, adventure, riddle, mystery, sacrifice, discovery, temptation, loss or gain of identity, metamorphosis, transformation, dragon-slaying, descent to an underworld, rebirth, redemption.* The *road up* and the *road down* is a common archetypal extension—an account of one who rises high but sinks low because of his or her own actions.

When an archetype is made flesh, how might it look? Let's make a quick run through some archetypal characters. It might be the hero: "Here I come to save the day." If that's all he amounts to, the hero will be one-dimensional, not quite believable, and not very interesting. The white-hat hero is reassuring to children, however, and should be a part of children's art. But the adult audience wants the perfect hero offstage as soon as he has swooped from the sky and cracked a few heads—that's his only identity and function. We don't see him at the supermarket or washing the car.

Unless he's Clark Kent. As every comic book fan knows, the godlike hero is more interesting if he has another and less perfect identity—Clark Kent *before* the phone booth. The superhero archetype gains dimension and layers by melding with other archetypes of character, theme, and action. Conflicting identity, in which characters are not at their cores what they seem on the surface, has been a storytelling staple since the gods moved incognito among earthlings. Characters of enduring interest often have layers and contradictions in identity. Ian Fleming's beloved hero is a multidimensional character in part because of the contradiction between the wise-cracking, womanizing, fashion-plate James Bond, and the dead earnest 007, a superhero who's there to save the day.

Another hero archetype is the flawed hero, which we've already discussed and which presents fertile ground for the writer. Some celebrated flawed heroes in Shakespeare are Hamlet (dithering and indecision), Macbeth (excessive ambition), Othello (jealousy and gullibility), and King Lear (naiveté).

And there's the anti-hero—pure badness and purely interesting. The anti-hero creates half the necessary tension between "white hats" and "black hats"—between good and evildoers. Think of Shakespeare's Iago and the generations of captivated audiences who have asked *why is he doing this?*

But the anti-hero represents evil, not insanity. The question *why is he doing this* asks for reason and motive. If the answer is that the character is *insane*, the character loses dimension and the audience loses interest. Like the happenstance act of nature or act of god, insanity is its own answer—there's nothing to learn from it. We see this in life as well as art. When a heinous criminal is seen simply to be mad, the public in essence shrugs and walks away. There's nothing left to say; nothing to wonder about; the over-arching question dies.

Extremist personalities—the possessed, obsessed, and compulsive—also are common archetypes. This archetype is an enriched version of the tragic hero: They may know what they're doing is wrong, but *they can't stop*. Think of *Moby Dick's* Captain Ahab, who can't stop his vengeful pursuit of the White Whale who left him with one leg and so finally goes with him to the ocean's depths. The extremist archetype may reflect some awful excess. Al Pacino's "Scarface" is an example. Such tales often demonstrate the hazards of excess as well as the virtues of moderation. Dante's Rings of Hell punish excess, for example, even that of gluttony.

The virtuous but abused "princess" archetype is omnipresent in art and is sometimes paired with the themes of lost or preserved innocence, as well as captivity, escape, and rescue.

The earth mother archetype is the enduring fecund protector and caretaker prominent in many archetypal tales.

The underdog, outcast, or rebel also is a common character archetype.

The Cinderella archetype is represented by a commoner, male or female, who becomes real or figurative royalty. We find this archetype in such tales as *The Prince and the Pauper*, along with other potent archetypes such as adventure, metamorphosis, identity, coming of age, and discovery. Rags-to-riches and Horatio Alger tales often reflect the Cinderella archetype as well.

The clown, fool, and trickster are figures that provide comic relief and perspective. They often comment on the action and point out hypocrisy or foolishness. Fools are "fools" only in antic or appearance; they may in fact be philosophers or have a certain wisdom. (Think of many Shakespearean fools, or of Forrest Gump in the movie of the same name.) Here's the idea, again, of things not being what they seem. Contradiction and complement are deeply satisfying in storytelling, as I suggested earlier—in part because complementary halves approach the *yin* and *yang* of wholeness.

We've seen how the archetype might function in art—now let's look at how it might function in life. Consider two riveting stories from the late 20th century: O.J. Simpson and Princess Diana. Many were bewildered by the hold these stories had on the public, but each was a potent amalgam of archetypes.

Simpson was a hero turned anti-hero and pariah. He was a charismatic black man of celebrity, charm, promise, and physical prowess who married a beautiful white woman and then was accused of killing her out of sexual jealousy. This is, of course, *Othello*, a Shakespearean tragedy that has captivated audiences for more than 400 years. And Shakespeare himself borrowed the story from a much earlier Italian tale—in short, it's an ancient drama. Unlike Othello, Simpson didn't kill himself, but in that farcical slow chase in the white Bronco, he threatened to do so. If he had, it would have been life imitating art perfectly.

Archetypally, Princess Diana was an even more complex composite. In her, we saw both the princess and Cinderella archetypes. After her transformation, she represented not only the fairy princess betrayed by a cruel husband and mistreated by a "wicked" queen, but also unrequited love, gain and loss of identity, metamorphosis, and escape. For years, she was tireless in a quest; she wanted her true prince, the one she thought she had married. Her early history flirted with archetypes of the possessed and obsessed and, later, with underdog, rebel, and outcast archetypes. And through it all, Diana was a model for motherhood, reflecting the earth mother archetype.

No wonder she stuck in the public's imagination. She was much more than celebrity or royalty—she was flesh-and-blood *story*. The world has many celebrities and royal figures, but there are few Dianas among them. That explains in part the world's paroxysm of grief over her death. Some asked why this great suffering over Diana but not over Mother Teresa, who died about the same time and was after all a noble and saintly person with none of Diana's personal flaws. They thought the outpouring of grief over Diana demonstrated the public's shallowness. It didn't. It demonstrated the public's love of *story*.

We've already discussed the fact that saintliness alone is not interesting. It's true that Diana was damaged and needy, and that she made mistakes. But many saw that humanity and identified with it—there's power in the story in which the audience sees itself. Few could see themselves in Mother Teresa, however, whose story held no tension, no fatal flaw, no hazard.

Further and equally important, Mother Teresa's story was told; Diana's was not. Mother Teresa died an old woman and of natural causes; Diana died young and violently. Mother Teresa's promise was fulfilled; Diana was a character still in conflict, and her audience awaited the dénouement. The last words Diana spoke to the press: "You won't believe what I'm going to do now."

What was it? No one will ever know. So we can add *riddle* to Diana's archetypal mix.

Remembering that *narrative* means *to know*, writers will better tell their tales if they understand the archetypal trappings of story and character. They'll know better how to shape and organize the story, what matters and what doesn't. Understanding the archetype means we can harness its considerable strength and use it to drive our story forward.

CHAPTER 14

Storytelling: The Narrative Engine

A Literary Analysis of a 'Real-Life' Story

He [the writer] must teach himself that the basest of all things is to be afraid; and, teaching himself that, forget it forever, leaving no room in his workshop for anything but the old verities and truths of the heart, the old universal truths lacking which any story is ephemeral and doomed—love and honor and pity and pride and compassion and sacrifice.
—William Faulkner, upon receiving the Nobel Prize

Below is a true story that is much more than reportage. It skillfully capitalizes on narrative writing as well as on archetypes, symbols, and other literary devices. It's a prizefight column written by David Casstevens, who was at the time a sports columnist for *The Dallas Morning News*. The work is brilliant, not least because it was written on an extremely tight deadline—it had to be finished shortly after the fight in order to appear in the newspaper the next morning. Despite time pressure, however, the column unrolls an orderly and unified narrative that represents good storytelling.

Writers sometimes employ such literary devices as archetype, symbol, foreshadowing, and symbolism without conscious intent. Such devices spring in part from artistic instinct.

But whether deliberate or instinctive, those devices enrich the story and add scope, purpose, drama, and meaning.

This piece's archetypal bones: Bubba, the hometown hero, is an underdog and a nobody. He is on a quest—he wants to prove himself, make a name for himself. (Quest archetypes often involve a search for success, recognition, identity, security, a coming of age, etc.) To fulfill his dream, he must face and slay a dragon, in the form of "the Champ." Awaiting the outcome is the golden-haired princess Kim.

Win or lose, this would be a good story: "Underdog Victorious!" Or "Underdog Defeated!" Either would have a more interesting story line than "Champ Wins!"

Here's Casstevens' column, followed by a paragraph-by-paragraph analysis of literary and archetypal device.

Bubba Busceme had big plans for his sweetheart. After he won the world lightweight title, he and Kim were going to spend a week in Acapulco. His $50,000 paycheck—the biggest of his life—was just the beginning. As the new champion, he could make seven or eight times that amount every time he defended his title.

'I'll be able to give Kim everything,' Bubba said the other day. 'I'll finally be able to make it so good for me and her, for the rest of our lives.'

Bubba and wife Kim are very much in love, which made the thought of waking up Sunday morning on top of the world just all that much sweeter. This was going to be a very special Valentine's Day.

So when her husband, the hometown hero, climbed into the ring Saturday and waved to 6,500 friends who chanted 'Bubba! Bubba!' Kim Busceme flushed with the mixed emotions of a bride-to-be. She was giddy with excitement and pride. She was nervous. And she was scared to death.

She'd met Bubba three years ago when she was working at a men's clothing store in Beaumont. They married two months later. Since their wedding, she'd never seen her husband lose a fight. He'd won 11 in a row. As he liked to say, Kim brought out the best in him.

She sat in a folding chair at ringside, not more than five feet from Bubba's corner. A slender, demure woman with long blond hair, 21-year-old Kim clutched a red heart-shaped satin pillow trimmed with lace her mother had made for her as a Valentine's Day gift. She looked out of place at a prizefight. This was a boisterous, beer-drinking crowd. A cigar-smoking crowd. Ringsiders were placing bets. Some were giving odds on how long Bubba would last. She was blood-splattering close to the ring, where her Bubba and Champion Alexis Arguello stood face to face. One man would fight for honor, the other for a dream.

Kim Busceme will remember the 24 minutes that followed as the longest of her life. As everyone had feared, Arguello stalked Busceme from the opening bell. He repeatedly backed his opponent into a corner. A master craftsman of his trade, Arguello never lost his poise. He never showed a trace of emotion. His face was as blank as an unaddressed envelope. He was a machine, patient but relentless.

Arguello used his 7-inch reach advantage well. For the first five rounds, the tall, lean champion stalked the 10-to-1 underdog and stockpiled points with a salvo of snake-licking left jabs and left hooks. He kept his right hand cocked near his ear. This was the same fearsome right that had scored 59 KOs in his 73 pro victories. The same right that broke Roberto Elizondo's jaw and rib in Arguello's last title defense in November.

Busceme, a southpaw, is a crafty fighter. He fights in flurries. He dodges punches well. He sniffs danger like a woods animal. But except for the opening round, when he was pumped sky-high with emotion, Bubba was no match for the 29-year-old champ, who turned pro at 14.

Perhaps Kim sensed the end was near going into the sixth round. She probably saw it on the face of Hugh Benbow, Busceme's manager. Between each round, the old man, aided by a cane, slowly climbed the steps and stuck his head between the ropes to offer words of instruction and encouragement to his fighter.

Bubba was still ahead on courage and heart, but he was badly behind on points.

Finally, the end came. Late in round six, Arguello caught Bubba's jaw with a brutal left hook. The crowd groaned like an old mattress. Shaken, his defenses down, Busceme didn't have time to react as the champ moved in with a right, and then with a left-right combination.

Bubba didn't know if he was in Beaumont or on Bourbon Street. 'I hardly remember anything after that,' he would say later. In a stumbling half-trot, he weaved drunkenly toward his corner. His mouth was open. His eyes were glass. The slightest push and he'd have fallen over like a storefront mannequin. Kim put her hand to her lips. Then, as the referee stepped in to stop the fight, she laid her head on the table in front of her and began to cry softly. Sobbing, her shoulders shaking, she never saw Bubba's cornermen rush into the ring to rescue their fallen fighter. She refused to look up. Hands trembling, she peeled from the table a 3-by-5 card with 'Kim Busceme' printed on it . . . .

Later, Busceme forced a smile when asked about his future. 'I'd like to box some more,' said Bubba, who turns 30 Sunday, on Valentine's Day. 'There's only one Alexis Arguello. But I feel I can box with any of the other guys.'

Kim looked at the floor. She still held her heart-shaped pillow. 'I wish he'd quit,' she murmured, her eyes welled with tears. 'I love him so much. But I don't think I can go through this again.'

The paragraph-by-paragraph analysis:

1) Bubba Busceme had big plans for his sweetheart. After he won the world lightweight title, he and Kim were going to spend a week in Acapulco. His $50,000 paycheck—the biggest of his life—was just the beginning. As the new champion, he could make seven or eight times that amount every time he defended his title.

2) 'I'll be able to give Kim everything,' Bubba said the other day. 'I'll finally be able to make it so good for me and her, for the rest of our lives.'

Foreshadowing in the opening sentence: Bubba *had* big plans (something went wrong). The rest of the paragraph also foreshadows and is heavy in irony: *after he won, his purse would be just the beginning, as the new champion.* Dramatic irony is the contrast between what a character thinks or says and what the audience knows to be the truth.

Notice that Casstevens does not say Bubba lost the fight; he introduces him, makes us care about him, then *shows* us his loss. (Remember that readers already knew Bubba lost the fight; it had happened the night before and had been in the news. Stories whose conclusions are known involve the reader's "willing suspension of disbelief"—they read as if they did not know the end. They're in it for the story, for the *how did it happen.*)

Making us care about Bubba involves selective story-telling, selective detail. The point of view will shift from Bubba to Kim, but it will always be from Bubba's corner. The Champ won't get equal time or treatment because the audience mustn't care about him. That would not only split the story's focus, it would also dilute the audience's interest in Bubba.

3) Bubba and wife Kim are very much in love, which made the thought of waking up Sunday morning on top of the world just all that much sweeter. This was going to be a very special Valentine's Day.

More foreshadowing, irony, and the introduction of a key symbol: Valentine's Day. This symbol is strengthened later when Kim appears clutching the heart-shaped pillow and when we learn that Valentine's Day is also Bubba's birthday. The column ran on Valentine's Day and emphasizes romance. (Reinforcing this imagery is the *sweetheart* of the opening sentence, *bride-to-be*, waking up together on Sunday morning, etc.)

115

4) So when her husband, the hometown hero, climbed into the ring Saturday and waved to 6,500 friends who chanted 'Bubba! Bubba!' Kim Busceme flushed with the mixed emotions of a bride-to-be. She was giddy with excitement and pride. She was nervous. And she was scared to death.

That paragraph presents a pivotal shift in point of view—from Bubba to Kim, where it will remain. We begin to see what Bubba represents to Kim: He is heroic rather than fallible. As we will learn shortly, she has never seen him lose.

More selective detail: 6,500 of "Bubba's friends" are cheering him. Is no one cheering for the Champ? Of course, but this is *Bubba's* story, and the effective storyteller will keep the camera on him, not his adversary. In the whole of this piece, we will not hear the Champ speak, nor meet his wife, his manager, his fans.

5) She'd met Bubba three years ago when she was working at a men's clothing store in Beaumont. They married two months later. Since their wedding, she'd never seen her husband lose a fight. He'd won 11 in a row. As he liked to say, Kim brought out the best in him.

Foreshadowing and irony: "She'd never seen her husband lose a fight." The reader is thinking: *She will now.* "Kim brought out the best in him." *Not this time.*

6) She sat in a folding chair at ringside, not more than five feet from Bubba's corner. A slender, demure woman with long blond hair, 21-year-old Kim clutched a red heart-shaped satin pillow trimmed with lace her mother had made for her as a Valentine's Day gift. She looked out of place at a prizefight. This was a boisterous, beer-drinking crowd. A cigar-smoking crowd. Ringsiders were placing bets; some were giving odds on how long Bubba would last. She was blood-splattering close to the ring, where her Bubba and Champion Alexis Arguello stood face to face. One man would fight for honor, the other for a dream.

In this pivotal paragraph, we meet the Champ for the first time, but he is presented as a symbol, an obstacle. He will fight to retain his title, but we don't know his story, his dream.

What are we told about Kim and what archetype does she reflect? She is young, innocent, naive, and vulnerable. Her mother made her the heart-shaped pillow she clutches, like a child with a stuffed toy. (*Clutch* is exactly the right word here. Kim's heartshaped pillow suggests both "wearing her heart on her sleeve" and dependence.) Kim suggests the princess/daughter archetype: fragile, emotionally dependent, protected. Is she brave, resilient? We don't know. But if she is *not*, she may be damaged by what she is about to see, a threat the reader senses. The references to beer, cigars, and blood underline Kim's vulnerability as an archetypal stranger in a strange land ("she looked out of place")—a position of learning, growth, and change, but also of possible danger ("she was blood-splattering close to the ring").

Consider: "Where her Bubba and champion Alexis Arguello stood face to face." Here, from time immemorial, is the obligatory confrontation between hero and nemesis. Character-conflict-resolution drama mandates this contest between adversaries. It could be a shootout on a dusty Wild West street, where the hero—spurs jangling, hand poised near his six-shooter—finally meets bad Black Bart. It could be a swashbuckler's final clash of sword. Or Sherlock meeting Moriarty. Whatever the form, the audience expects a showdown; it provides the story's climax.

7) Kim Busceme will remember the 24 minutes that followed as the longest of her life. As everyone had feared, Arguello stalked Busceme from the opening bell. He repeatedly backed his opponent into a corner. A master craftsman of his trade, Arguello never lost his poise. He never showed a trace of emotion. His face was as blank as an unaddressed envelope. He was a machine, patient but relentless.

Now we learn something about the Champ. As Casstevens portrays him, he is a machine, which presents yet another archetype—man vs. machine and loss of humanity. The Champ is shown as a bloodless automaton, a *terminator*.

Notice the words, "As *everyone* had feared." Is this true? No. The Champ had his fans and supporters, too. The effect of that small word *everyone* puts all of us with the underdog and against the Champ.

> *8) Arguello used his 7-inch reach advantage well. For the first five rounds, the tall, lean champion stalked the 10-to-1 underdog and stockpiled points with a salvo of snake-licking left jabs and left hooks. He kept his right hand cocked near his ear. This was the same fearsome right that had scored 59 KOs in his 73 pro victories. The same right that broke Roberto Elizondo's jaw and rib in Arguello's last title defense in November.*

That paragraph sets up the "force-of-nature" device, an unbeatable weapon that will vanquish our hero—who, after all, is only *human*. Bubba's humanity is further reinforced by the following paragraph:

> *9) Busceme, a southpaw, is a crafty fighter. He fights in flurries. He dodges punches well. He sniffs danger like a woods animal. But except for the opening round, when he was pumped sky-high with emotion, Bubba was no match for the 29-year-old champ, who turned pro at 14.*

Contrary to the impersonal and mechanistic imagery describing the Champ, the language describing Bubba reinforces his flesh-andblood identity: *crafty, sniffs danger like a woods animal, pumped sky-high with emotion.*

10) Perhaps Kim sensed the end was near going into the sixth round. She probably saw it on the face of Hugh Benbow, Busceme's manager. Between each round, the old man, aided by a cane, slowly climbed the steps and stuck his head between the ropes to offer words of instruction and encouragement to his fighter.

Do you recognize an archetype in Hugh Benbow? It is common for the hero or heroine to have a mentor, someone who trains, advises, and aids. The mentor is so common in art and myth that Joseph Campbell terms it the "wise old man" or "wise old woman" figure.

11) Bubba was still ahead on courage and heart, but he was badly behind on points.

Courage and *heart* again reinforce Bubba's flesh-and-blood aspect. The paragraph says, in effect, that Bubba is ahead in humanity but behind in mechanistic technicality.

12) Finally, the end came. Late in round six, Arguello caught Bubba's jaw with a brutal left hook. The crowd groaned like an old mattress. Shaken, his defenses down, Busceme didn't have time to react as the champ moved in with a right, and then with a left-right combination.

What is Cassteven's adjective for the left hook that brings Bubba down? *Brutal*. Is it? No. But that's how it seems to Bubba's supporters. What's the crowd's reaction? It "groaned like an old mattress." Again, that's selective detailing.

13) Bubba didn't know if he was in Beaumont or on Bourbon Street. 'I hardly remember anything after that,' he would say later. In a stumbling half-trot, he weaved drunkenly toward his corner. His mouth was open. His eyes were glass. The slightest push and he'd have fallen over like a storefront mannequin.

With this scene, Bubba loses his humanity and becomes an automaton himself, less than human, eyes glass, a storefront mannequin.

> 14) *Kim put her hand to her lips. Then, as the referee stepped in to stop the fight, she laid her head on the table in front of her and began to cry softly. Sobbing, her shoulders shaking, she never saw Bubba's cornermen rush into the ring to rescue their fallen fighter. She refused to look up. Hands trembling, she peeled from the table a 3-by-5 card with 'Kim Busceme' printed on it . . . .*

What does it mean that Kim refused to see her hero defeated? That she refused to look? That she peeled her name from the table (*I wasn't here; I didn't see this*)? Does she hold her head high, try to meet his eyes, to reassure him with her own? She does not. She hides her face, shields her eyes, protects herself from the truth. In short, she *denies*.

> 15) *Later, Busceme forced a smile when asked about his future. 'I'd like to box some more,' said Bubba, who turns 30 Sunday, on Valentine's Day. 'There's only one Alexis Arguello. But I feel I can box with any of the other guys.'*

What of Bubba? He lost! Does he shrivel like a slice of bacon in a hot pan? No way. His words are not those of resignation or bitterness, but of hope and reconciliation. Sure, Bubba's disappointed, but his vision and survivor skills are intact: *Bummer, I lost. OK, then I'll adjust my dream, but I'll still have a dream. The champ may be the best right now, but I'm still good. I'll fight again.* This is the voice of wisdom and moderation, also commonly manifest in heroes. (Usually, such heroes redouble their efforts and return for a second contest, which they win.) Bubba will be fine.

And Kim, meantime?

16) Kim looked at the floor. She still held her heart-shaped pillow. 'I wish he'd quit,' she murmured, her eyes welled with tears. 'I love him so much. But I don't think I can go through this again.'

People commonly remark, reading this column, *I don't like the end*. Why? *Not sure, it unsettles me.*

Yes, and it should.

Who took the bigger hit tonight, Bubba or Kim? They both lost a dream, but it wasn't the same dream. He lost a fight; she lost her hero. So here she is, still holding her heart-shaped pillow, a remnant of illusion. Are her tears for Bubba, or for herself and her lost innocence? Does she say: *Bummer, you lost! But don't worry about it. You'll beat him next time.* She does not. She says: *Quit.* She says: *I don't think I can go through this again.* She says: *I love him so much.* And then there is that telltale *but.*

Of course that's an unsettling end. It creates a half-formed concern: Can Kim leave the princess behind and become a queen? Can she be a *mate* and live in the real world—or only a sweetheart, wrapped in illusion?

So. Did readers of the sports section that Sunday say: *Hey, look at this. Casstevens is using archetypal imagery, foreshadowing, and irony in this column.* No. But they felt the impact of those devices. They recognized the movement of *story*—the ancient archetypal patterns of quest, struggle, defeat, and reconciliation—and the story resonated. As the song says, the fundamental things apply, as time goes by.

CHAPTER 15

Building Interest and Suspense

Don't Say Everything. At Least Don't Say it Right Now.

The secret of being a bore is to tell everything.

—Voltaire

As the last two chapters suggest, a common and effective way of heightening reader interest is to create a question in the reader's mind but delay answering it, or to evoke reader curiosity but delay satisfying it. The technique, commonly used in serial dramas, ends each segment at its highest point of drama and uncertainty, with an unanswered question or plot twist. The common question is *what's going to happen now?* Will Pauline—whom we last saw tied to the tracks as a train sped toward her—somehow survive?

The delayed answer in serializations is forced—the audience *must* wait until the next installment or segment to find out what happens. That same device works in other varieties of writing as well, once critical elements of the story line are established and the characters are introduced. You can force a pause, much as a serial forces pauses, by presenting the activities of multiple characters separately and in a loose sequence.

For example, in a segment involving Character A, you advance the plot by answering a question posed in an earlier

Character A segment. Then you pose a new question or create a new tension involving Character A and end the segment without answering that question or resolving that tension. In other words, you suspend A's narrative at that point and begin a new segment, which involves, say, Character B, whose story likewise was left hanging at the end of the last B segment. In this way, you lead readers through the work by repeatedly renewing their curiosity.

The segments interlock to complete the plot "puzzle." Segments can be separate, as in chapters or sections, or integrated into one narrative. Either way, they function the same. And those principles apply equally to nonfiction and fiction. They apply whenever we're writing a narrative—something with a storytelling beginning, middle, and end.

The brief newspaper excerpt below, from a gripping account of a murder written by journalist Mike Mather for the *Virginian-Pilot,* integrates parallel narratives. The story in part follows the actions of two detectives, Barber and Bynum. Each is told in segments separated by simple transitions rather than by more elaborate breaks.

> *Then the Norfolk crime lab called. It had raised the serial number on the revolver. Barber ordered a trace. He wasn't prepared for what it showed.*
> *Meanwhile, Bynum also was struggling.*

That excerpt illustrates one of Mather's transitions or bridges from one character's segment to another's. The curiosity-provoking words in this excerpt are "he wasn't prepared for what it showed." At this point, the readers are expecting to hear what Barber learned from the trace on the revolver. But the writer suspends Barber's investigation at this high point of reader interest, leaving it (and the reader) hanging and moving on to a Bynum segment—which repeats the process of building tension or curiosity.

With this time-honored "meanwhile, back at the ranch" technique, each segment ends when the reader's interest is highest, thus propelling the reader through the story. When readers say, "I couldn't put it down," it's usually because of unresolved issues or unanswered questions—they're eager to find out *what's going to happen next*.

Some cautions. Don't wait too long to deal with unresolved material, and don't have too many *significant* unanswered questions working at once, or the readers will become frustrated, even angry. Also, the device should not be obvious; in other words, the reader should experience *effect* rather than *device*. Finally, the unanswered question or unresolved issue must seem significant, interesting, even compelling. Otherwise, who cares if it's unanswered or unresolved?

Mystery writer Elizabeth George is a master of creating interest by leaving the reader hanging. The following passage ends a chapter in her novel, *A Traitor to Memory*.

> 'Why am I telling you?' Webberly didn't wait for a reply before he sank into a desk chair and said, 'Because of the victim, Tommy. She's Eugenie Davies, and I want you involved. I want to move heaven and earth and hell if I have to, to get to the bottom of what happened to her. Leach knew that the moment he saw who she was.'
>
> Lynley frowned. 'Eugenie Davies? Who was she?'
>
> 'How old are you, Tommy?'
>
> 'Thirty-seven, sir.'
>
> Webberly blew out a breath. 'Then I suppose you're too young to remember.'

That passage, which occurs early in the book, awakens curiosity about the slain woman as well as about Webberly's vehemence regarding her death. With his words, "Then I suppose you're too young to remember," he is announcing: *There's a story here.* And we're eager to hear it. But we must suspend our curiosity because the next chapter moves on to another character's narrative. Our curiosity is only suspended, however; it isn't gone—and its presence keeps us turning the pages. We know the author will return to the matter sooner or later.

Here's another chapter end from the same George novel:

> *One of the newer constables came barreling into the room. He was called Solberg, a wet-behind-the-ears DC who'd been eager to prove himself from day one on the murder squad. He was trailing a sheaf of paperwork behind him, and his face was so red, he looked like a runner at the end of a marathon.*
>
> *He cried out, 'Guv! Check this out. Ten days ago, and it's hot. It's hot.'*
>
> *Leach said, 'What are you on about, Solberg?'*
>
> *'A bit of a complication,' the constable replied.*

We want to know what that complication is, but again we must wait, because with those words, George moves on to another character. Here's yet another such passage from the same work:

> *'I've got him naming Pytches right here in my notes.'*
>
> *'Pytches?' Havers asked. 'No. it's not Pytches, Inspector. That can't—'*
>
> *Lynley's mobile rang. He grabbed it from the table top and held up a finger to stop Havers from continuing. She was itching to do so, however. She'd stubbed out her cigarette impatiently, saying 'What day did you talk to Davies, Inspector?'*
>
> *Lynley waved her off, clicked on his mobile, said, 'Lynley,' and turned away from Havers' smoke.*
>
> *His caller was DCI Leach. 'We've got another victim,' he announced.*

Two things build interest and suspense in that passage. We can see that Havers is bursting to tell the inspector something, and our own impatience grows with hers: We want to know what that something is. Then a call stops her mid-sentence and announces another victim—whose identity likewise is withheld. *Wait!* we want to cry as the narrative leaves that segment and moves on to another.

Elizabeth George is by no means the only mystery writer who has perfected the "leave-'em-wanting-more" device. The technique is a staple of the genre. Here, the much-honored British writer Ruth Rendel writes of a character named Vine in her novel *Simisola*:

> *Leaving Cousins's, he began his investigation of the market, and on the second stall he looked at he saw for sale a radio-cassette player. It was made of a hard white plastic substance and across the top of it, just above the digital clock, was a dark red stain someone had tried in vain to eradicate. For a moment or two Vine thought the stain was blood and then he remembered.*

That "then he remembered" is the same sort of dramatic device as George's "Then I suppose you're too young to remember." It's a preamble to a story: *Listen, my children, and you shall hear . . . .*

Withholding an answer or resolution is a natural tactic in murder mysteries, but the device works in any genre, whether fiction or nonfiction. Author Frances Mayes ends a chapter in her novel *Swan*: "Holt, after years and years, was not about to erode Catherine's trust. She never had betrayed his secret." That sentence creates curiosity because at this point the reader is thinking: *Secret? What secret?* It's human nature to want to *know*. Mayes keeps the secret a bit longer, though, forcing us to read on if we want to find out what the secret is. In other words, we're hooked.

Suggestion or insinuation, rather than stating outright, is another form of withholding that can provoke reader interest, both in fiction and nonfiction. The implicit is often more interesting than the explicit. And the time-honored device of foreshadowing can likewise create reader curiosity. In "Mrs. Kelly's Monster," a nonfiction newspaper feature that won the

Pulitzer Prize, author Jon Franklin begins with the following two paragraphs:

> *In the cold hours of a winter morning, Dr. Thomas Barbee Ducker, chief brain surgeon at the University of Maryland Hospital, rises before dawn. His wife serves him waffles but no coffee. Coffee makes his hands shake.*
>
> *In downtown Baltimore, on the 12th floor of University Hospital, Edna Kelly's husband tells her goodbye. For 57 years Mrs. Kelly shared her skull with the monster: No more.*

Jon Franklin does not say that Dr. Ducker will perform harrowing brain surgery on Edna Kelly this day, but juxtaposing those brief paragraphs suggests it—as do the pregnant words, "no more." Also, "coffee makes his hands shake" suggests that the surgeon's hands must not shake today.

Franklin, who has been called a master of the nonfiction short story, is also a master of compression, of not saying too much. His opening is rich in its restraint and sets the right mood immediately—in part because he knows not only what to say, but also what not to say. Regarding his opening words, "In the cold hours of a winter morning," Franklin says in his book *Writing for Story:* "Dr. Ducker also rose to a warm house and bright future, but those facts are not relevant to the story being told."

Early in the opening chapter of Kenneth Roberts' *Northwest Passage*, the author writes that although certain subjects may seem irrelevant, he must touch on all of them—for they "have a bearing on what happened later." He doesn't expand at that moment on *what happened later,* so we read the entire book to find out. It's an age-old story-telling device, this withholding, and the next chapter will further explore the value of not saying everything.

CHAPTER 16

Building Interest and Suspense

Let the Readers Do Some Work

You can say anything as long as it's true, but everything that's true is not worth saying.

—Stanley Kunitz

As we saw in the last chapter, people are interested in what we withhold as well as in what we reveal. Write that something is the second largest, or the third most popular, or the fourth leading cause of, and readers will immediately clamor: *What are the others?*

Obviously, withholding *information* in an informational report is unwise. And withholding must be judicious in any case. But a little well-planned withholding in creative work can enrich the work and build reader curiosity and interest. Dare not to explain everything, especially material most readers will know. One of the welcome differences between reports and stories is that reports often contain annoying footnotes or other documentation; stories generally do not.

Creative writers can strengthen their work with allusions or quotations, for example, without explaining or attributing them. This is especially true of quotations, if they're well known. Sometimes both writer and characters can have fun with allusions or quotations, or otherwise find them useful in clarifying the action. In Ruth Rendel's *Shake Hands Forever,* her sleuth Inspector Wexford says on the phone to one of his investigators: "Howard, you are my only ally." Howard responds: "Well, you know what Chesterton said about that. I'll be at that bus stop from five-thirty onwards tonight and then we'll see." Rendel continues:

> *Wexford put on his dressing gown and went downstairs to find what Chesterton had said. 'There are no words to express the abyss between isolation and having one ally. It may be conceded to the mathematicians that four is twice two. But two is not twice one; two is two thousand times one . . . .' He felt considerably cheered. Maybe he had no force of men at his disposal but he had Howard, the resolute, the infinitely reliable, the invincible, and together they were two thousand.*

Pertinent as Chesterton's words are to Wexford's situation, it would be awkward for Rendel herself to use them. By giving the allusion to a character instead, she maintains her invisibility as a narrator while telling the reader something about the characters, their interests, and relationship as well. The allusion, and Wexford's reaction, also helps the reader understand Wexford's state of mind.

In Rendel's Wexford mysteries, the inspector is well read and sometimes quotes authors who are either not identified or not identified right away. The quotations are apt and meaningful whether or not they're attributed, and the reader learns to trust that if it matters, we will find out whose words they are.

The trick is not to annoy readers with the unexplained: Either it does not matter or the allusion contains its own explanation. For example, we could safely write: "A modern-day Icarus, he tried flying and fell to the earth." We do not have to stop and recount the Icarus myth in order for the reader to understand the reference: *Whoever* Icarus was, he experimented with flying and fell from the sky. Likewise, we could safely write, without explaining who W.C. Fields was: "Like W.C. Fields, she hated children and animals." Again, most readers will know about Fields, but those who don't will know that whoever he was, he hated children and animals. Obviously, the world is richer for those who can pick apart layers of meaning. The unexplained allusion is sort of a subterranean communication between writer and reader—a salute to a world of shared information. The reader who recognizes an allusion is twice blessed, but the reader who doesn't recognize will still understand it if it is carefully presented.

Understanding the value of leaving things unsaid can force writers to find ways of *showing instead of telling*—one of the most important and time-honored tenets of good writing. There's no more effective practitioner of that principle than Elmore Leonard. Leonard has few equals in creating compelling characters, engaging dialogue, and tight, show-instead-of-tell prose. He often skips transitions and incorporates characterization and description into his narrative and dialogue. He is especially effective in not saying everything, in leaving something for readers to understand or imagine. He explains his unusual economy by saying: "I try to keep out the parts that people skip."

Leonard's skill for compression, elliptical dialogue, and for showing instead of telling is seen in the following typically revealing and amusing excerpt from his novel *Cuba Libre*. The book is set in 1898 Cuba at a time when the USS Maine has been sabotaged, the *insurrectos* wait in the hills, and Teddy Roosevelt's Rough Riders are about to come ashore.

In this passage, Rudi Calvo, who has been tailing the book's main character Ben Tyler, reports to police chief Andres Palenzuela, who suspects Tyler of being a U.S. agent. Calvo's report is far more cloak than dagger, though, because it concerns our rough-and-tough hero on a shopping spree for fancy new clothes. In presenting this discussion between Calvo and Palenzuela, Leonard portrays Ben Tyler through their eyes rather than through his own—through dialogue rather than through authorial description. In so doing, he not only reveals something interesting about the main character, but also about Calvo and Palenzuela. Again, the book is set in a dangerous time, involving dangerous characters and dangerous activity. Yet, Calvo's is a thorough report on what should be shallow and beside the point, given the climate and Palenzuelo's position as chief of police. And Palenzuelo, for his part, is captivated rather than annoyed. Watch him become less interested in Ben Tyler's suspected undercover activity than in his wardrobe. Leonard doesn't tell us that Palenzuelo is a dandy, a "man of fashion"; he lets us discover that for ourselves through Palenzuelo's questions and responses.

> *At 9:00 p.m. Rudi Calvo came to the home in the Vedado suburb of Havana where Palenzuelo kept his American mistress—her name was Lorraine—and entertained close friends. Rudi sat with his chief in the front courtyard of the house to give his report.*
>
> *'From the ferry dock the subject went directly to the Hotel Inglaterra, where he registered and left his belongings, a bedroll and a saddle. He spent almost two hours in the bar among the newspaper correspondents before going out again. His associate, the one named Burke, remained.'*
>
> *He had caught Palenzuela getting dressed for the evening, suspenders hanging, buttoning his shirt, a collar not yet attached, the chief's mind apparently on something else, the reason he said, 'Who?'*
>
> *'Charlie Burke,' Rudi said, always patient with his chief, and explained that they already had a file on Burke, a dealer in cattle who had been here several times before. 'The subject went out again accompanied by Victor Fuentes and proceeded to la Habana Vieja, where they dined in a café and then visited stores, selecting new clothes for the subject. Shirts, trousers, a suit coat, good boots and a very fine Panama.'*
>
> *'He bought a suit?' Palenzuela said.*
>
> *'Only the coat, a black one.'*
>
> *'Expensive?'*

'I believe alpaca.'

'Where did he go for the boots?'

'Naranjo y Vasquez.'

'They're all right, but not the best.'

'He removed his spurs from the old boots and put them on the new ones.'

'Why? If he wasn't riding?'

'No, I think because he's used to wearing them. Or he likes to hear himself walk.'

'A cowboy,' Palenzuela said. 'And where did he buy his hat?'

'Viadero's.'

'Of course.'

'He put on the clothes, the black suit coat and pants the color of sand, or perhaps more of a cinnamon shade.'

'How did it look?'

'Elegant, with a white shirt and a kerchief of a light blue shade, the kerchief his own.'

Palenzuela said, 'Hmmmm,' nodding. 'I like a kerchief sometimes.'

'He had something he brought with him wrapped in newspaper,' Rudi Calvo said. 'I had been wondering, what is that he's carrying? Well, he unwrapped it now in the store. It was a revolver, I believe a Smith & Wesson .44, the one with the spur beneath the trigger guard for the second finger.'

'The .44 Russian,' Palenzuela said, 'originally designed for a grand duke. I have a pair.'

'He carried it,' Rudi said, 'in a shoulder holster.'

'If he isn't a spy,' Palenzuela said, 'he could be an assassin.'

That amusing conversation shows us *dudes*, Leonard style. Particularly revealing is Calvo's meticulous description of Tyler's new pants—" sand, or maybe more of a cinnamon shade"—as well as Palenzuelo's "I like a kerchief sometimes" and, speaking of a revolver designed for a grand duke, "I have a pair."

Small questions or curiosities often seduce Leonard's readers. The following passage is from his novel *Bandits*. The book's hero, Jack, snoops through the private correspondence of an adversary, a Nicaraguan. He finds a letter from Ronald Reagan, the final paragraph of which reads:

> *I have requested my friends . . . to give you a generous leg up, that you may ride to victory over communism. I have asked them to help you carry the fight through their support, and come to realize in their hearts, 'no es pesado, es mi hermano.'*

Leonard does not translate that last for the non-Spanish-speaking readers; he lets both Jack and the reader wonder—for nearly 60 pages. Withholding that little bit allows Leonard to return to it later and along the way to show how Jack thinks and works—independently and patiently:

> *That closing, in Spanish, Jack had figured out to mean 'he isn't heavy, he's my . . . .'*
> *In the silence, concentrating, he heard the sounds coming from the other room. The key in the lock. Someone coming in, trying to, pushing on the door but having trouble with it. Trying again now. Jack picked up the Beretta from the desk.*

Leonard doesn't finish the translated quotation with the word *brother*, because he doesn't have to—it's so well known that finishing it would be trite if not insulting. So he says just enough to clue the reader, then brings an intruder onstage to keep him from having to say more.

The principle of saying just enough, vital to effective writing, is mirrored by the principle of *showing* just enough. And the purpose of showing (instead of telling) is to recreate reality through description.

That's the subject of the next chapter.

CHAPTER 17

Description: Creating Word Pictures

Quick, Get the Camera

Words, when well chosen, have so great a force in them that a description often gives us more lively ideas than the sight of things themselves.

—Playwright Joseph Addison

Good writers know how to describe people, places, things, and actions so that the reader can see them too. They create pictures with words. And because carefully chosen words carry great force, word pictures are often stronger than the sight of the real thing.

Crafting description plagues many writers, but it shouldn't. Any writer worth a darn should be able to write decent description. Yet we too often read awful descriptions, and from professional writers. The worst description I ever read was by a best-selling novelist who sized up World War II this way: "The war was just terrible."

Well . . . *yes.*

Why is that breathless and empty sentence so bad, aside from being idiotically simplistic? It's bad because it offers no real information. It brings to mind an amusing sentence from a student writer's composition: "His vocabulary was so small it was like *whatever.*"

The tenets of effective description are easy to grasp and execute: Good description is fast, spare, specific, and showing. Weak description is slow, wordy, vague, abstract, and telling. The distinction between showing and telling is particularly important. Telling fails to create an immediate and vivid mental image—it simply offers a conclusion, which readers may find difficult to accept because it's not *their* conclusion. Showing, on the other hand, creates a perfectly focused picture that is both vivid and direct.

What might you write if you were asked to describe popcorn to someone who had never seen or tasted it? Uncooked kernels of a special kind of corn that explode when heated? That *tells* us popcorn, but it doesn't *show* us popcorn—it captures nothing of the popcorn "experience," its buttery, salty taste, the feel of it on the tongue, its characteristic and unique smell, its associations. For all that, you need the senses—and you need showing words.

Consider: "At the end of the road, on the bank of the Rio Batopilas, is Batopilas, a fascinating old village of picturesque houses and narrow lanes." In that passage, the telling words *fascinating, old,* and *picturesque* do little to help the reader see the scene. But specific, showing words can bring the scene to life: *At road's end, the stucco haciendas and cobblestone lanes of the antique village Batopilas lie nestled on the bank of the Rio Batopilas.*

In the following example, *white paint* and *onion-domes* create a picture, but *impressive structure* does not: "An impressive structure, with its white paint and red onion-domes, stands in a valley in the mountains." We need concrete information about that "impressive structure" before we can see it. Maybe: *A huge Byzantine cathedral, its fresh white paint punctuated by red onion-domes, gleams in the mountain valley.*

Consider: "The sunrise was strikingly beautiful." We'd have to know exactly what the writer found "strikingly beautiful" before we could see that sunrise: *The sun rose in a blaze of red and violet and gold.*

Notice the use of active verbs rather than static verbs in the description revisions. Active verbs are showing verbs: The village *nestles* on the bank rather than *is* on the bank. The cathedral *gleams* in the valley rather than *stands* in the valley. The sun *rose* rather than the sunrise *was*.

Incorporating action verbs into the description—particularly when describing people—can keep the passage from seeming inert. For example: "His countenance seemed owlish, in part because of his low and heavy browline." Bringing active verbs into that description energizes it: *He sent her an owlish glance from beneath a heavy, low-hanging brow.*

"He chewed tobacco constantly—Redman was his favorite brand." Revised: *His cheek bulged with the ever-present plug of Redman.* That bulging cheek makes a picture that shows us more than "he chewed tobacco."

"He was obviously near-sighted, judging from how near he held the menu, and his nose was large and hooked—more like a beak than a nose." Revised: *He brought the menu to within several inches of his beak-like nose.*

Although showing is more compelling than telling, the most full and satisfying description combines the two, as does the following passage from John McPhee's *Coming into the Country.* The passage, a marvel of clarity, records not only what McPhee sees, but also how he sees it:

> *Something in the general drift now has John Kauffmann on his feet and off to the river. He assembles his trout rod, threads its eyes. Six feet three, spare, he walks, in his determination, tilted forward, ten degrees from vertical, jaws clamped. He seems to be seeking reassurance from the river. He seems not so much to want to catch what may become the last grayling in Arctic Alaska as to certify that it is there. With his bamboo rod, his lofted line, he now describes long drape folds in the air above the river. His shirt is old and red. There are holes in his felt hat and strips of spare rawhide around its crown. He agitates the settled fly. Nothing. Again he waves the line. He drops its passenger on the edge of fast water at the far side of the pool. There is a vacuum-implosive sound,*

a touch of violence at the surface of the river. We cheer. For two minutes, we wait it out while Kauffmann plays his fish. Adroitly, gingerly, he brings it in. With care, he picks it up. He then looks at us as if he is about to throw his tin star in the dust at our feet. Shame—for our triple-hooked lures, our nylon hawsers, our subsequent stories of fished-out streams. He looks at his grayling. It is a twenty-five-ounce midget, but it will grow. He seems to feel reassured. He removes the fly, which has scarcely nicked the fish's lips. He slips the grayling back into the stream.

Interspersed among McPhee's telling statements (Kauffman's height and build, his hat and shirt, his actions) are showing statements (Kauffmann *seems* to be seeking reassurance, he *seems* not so much to want to catch the last grayling, he looks *as if* he is about to throw his tin star in the dust).

Some non-fiction writers are uneasy about crafting description—especially interpretive description—apparently fearing that it may be out of place in factual writing. But as McPhee demonstrates, showing description is as appropriate to factual writing as it is to fiction—and sometimes it's a great relief from starchy just-the-facts-ma'am writing.

Here are a handful of journalists with sure descriptive powers. Anthony DePalma, writing for *The New York Times*, could have said that so-called "oxygen salons"—bars that sell you a jolt of O2—offer some absurd images. He shows us instead:

Dressed in a deep-green bodysuit and wraparound sunglasses, blond hair pulled up like a pineapple on her head, Ann Marie Murphy was not the least bit self-conscious about sitting at a bar with a hose up her nose.

Likewise, Michelle Boorstein, writing for The Associated Press, lets description capture the absurd in a story about a mayoral candidate in Mesa, Arizona—a city known for conservative politics. The candidate was Kat Gallant, who among other things ran a massage parlor. In the following passage, she finishes a haircut and sends her client off to the back of the salon for his massage:

> *. . . to a room that soon emits giggles and wafts of body oil. Creaking slightly in her black leather leotard, Gallant slips off her stiletto heels and gets comfortable on the couch. It's time to talk politics.*

Consider how the senses bring that amusing description to life. There's sight, of course. And touch (the massage). Smell (wafts of fragrant oil). Sound (the creaking leather leotard).

Here's Christopher Reynolds, writing for the *Los Angeles Times:*

> *By night, the stars shine brightly, and below you can pick out the slowly but steadily advancing lights of ships as they transit the canal. Meanwhile, to the west, the skyscrapers of Panama City twinkle.*

And Steve Hendrix, writing for *The Washington Post,* describes a Gray Line tour bus:

> *. . . carrying visitors to sights mentioned in the best-selling book* Midnight in the Garden of Good and Evil. *Many of the bus' windows are down; lenses bristle like cannon barrels through open gun ports. A muffled, metallic voice declaims the rich history of this antique graveyard.*

In the following passage, the late Russell Smith of *The Dallas Morning News* might have told us that his subject typified a British rock star. Instead, he shows us.

> *The hair is a mess, the familiar jet-black rooster cut reduced to a confused, slept-on snarl. The chalky-white complexion shows no signs of ever having seen sunlight. A whopper of a*

nose dominates the long, rubbery face, and he looks almost like
a caricature of the quintessential British rock star.
He looks great. Like a Rolling Stone.

Here's a picture of distance runners created for *The Dallas Morning News* by sports columnist David Casstevens:

> *You've seen them on TV. Lank of frame, painters' caps on*
> *their heads, they go strutting out of the stadium shortly after*
> *dawn and aren't heard from again for two days, when they*
> *finally reappear in the arena, arms pumping, elbows rotating,*
> *still heel-toeing to beat the band, looking no worse for wear*
> *than when they left.*

One of the things that makes all those passages work is that they're fast and spare. We should mercilessly cut clutter and compress for two reasons: Description can be a space-eater and overlong description has few rivals in tedium. Even brief passages are damaged by clutter: "Topped by a yellow dome, the blue tower peeks from the forest ceiling like a stray golf ball perched on a blue tee in an epic rough." That sentence is plenty specific, and the verbs and images are active. But we can't see what the writer saw because he throws too many images at us.

John LeCarré is a master of both fresh description *and* compression. In the passage below, from *The Night Manager*, he identifies people by their clothing and presents most of the passage in fragment and suggestion:

> *After the camel hair came a navy blue blazer in his twen-*
> *ties, the blazer single-breasted for the cross-draw, and eyes*
> *shallow as paint . . . .*
>
> *'Been here long then, Pine? Wasn't here last time round,*
> *was he, Frisky? We'd have noticed a stray young Brit.'*
>
> *'No way,' said the blazer, eyeing Jonathan through an*
> *imaginary gun slit. Cauliflower ears, Jonathan noticed. Blond*
> *hair, going on white. Hands like axheads.*

Inventive descriptions of people are especially challenging, but everything we've said so far applies—with the added caution that triteness is a special hazard when describing personal appearance. We've read so many descriptions of people that the ready cliché comes leaping to mind—hair like silk, like wheat, like spun gold, like a raven's wing. Lips like cherries, cheeks like roses . . . . But LeCarré's similes above are fresh and original creations that bring the character to life. Once, after reviewing yet another effort from an author of potboilers, I suddenly realized that the writer had given all her heroes an unruly swath of hair that fell over their foreheads and all her heroines "endlessly long legs." Now, near book's end, she seemed confused by her own clichés—or maybe she was letting her computer copy and paste—because suddenly a man had endlessly long legs and a woman got the swath of hair.

Writers who specialize in fresh phrasing don't traffic in clichés. Peter De Vries' novels, which seldom repeat themselves, include a colonel who, when he laughed, showed "an octave of good teeth." De Vries also described a character as "thick-figured, thick-fingered, thick-necked, thick." And one of his characters mentions a "baked face with handsome features that included the diamond-shaped eyes of the Irish."

Novelist and *Dallas Morning News* reporter Doug Swanson also offers readers fresh looks at people. From his novel *Dreamboat:*

> *Roberts had a gray comb-over and one bad eye that drifted to the left.*
>
> *His brown beard was cut close over his cheeks, and he talked with a twang routed through his nose.*
>
> *The sheriff wore a khaki uniform starched to armorplate. He had black hair gelled straight back and mud-colored narrow eyes that looked Jack up and down without giving away anything. His skin was Hollywood bronze. He put Jack in mind of a ferret with a two-picture deal.*

Below, P.D. James describes a character in *Innocent Blood* named Harry Cleghorn:

He was strongly muscled, with a smooth, high-colored skin, hair so black that it looked dyed, and a moist, rather petulant mouth whose lips, red at the outlines as if lipsticked, revealed when he spoke an under-bleb of soft pale pink.

And a character in *A Certain Justice* named Edmund Albert Froggett:

The surname was almost ludicrously appropriate to that long, downturned mouth, those exophthalmic eyes. No doubt in childhood he must have suffered from the cruelty of the young and had somehow grown his defensive carapace of self-regard and slight pomposity. How else could the unfortunate of the world survive? Come to that, thought Dalgliesh, how could anyone? We none of us present ourselves psychologically naked to the barbs of the world.

Fresh, crisp, and compressed descriptions only *look* easy. They usually take considerable thought and multiple edits. Here's a brief "people" description from my own work as I originally wrote it and, then, as I rewrote it to make the words mesh better in sound and sense:

Original: We shook hands. His felt bony in mine, the flesh dry and cool. He was thinner and frailer than when I saw him in November and on that day wore baggy trousers and a roomy sweater that emphasized how slight he had become.

First revision: He was more frail than I remembered. He was gaunt in baggy gray cords and a loose black cardigan. He extended a bony hand, and his grip was dry and cool.

Final revision: He had become frail since November— baggy gray trousers hung on his hipbones, and an old black cardigan loosely draped his hollow chest. Shaking his hand was like clasping a bird's claw.

Read those three passages aloud so that both your ears and eyes work for you. How is the final version better description than the original? Let's look at the considerations that went into the passage's successive edits.

Original. This version makes and remakes the same point: *bony, thinner, frailer, slight.* Its focus splits unnecessarily to include the writer—*when I saw him in November,* and *felt bony in mine,* a near-redundancy. That handclasp: Could I *show* it instead of tell it? Also, the word *frailer,* although correct, seems awkward. And the description of the clothing could be more specific.

First revision. This version is tighter, but the first two sentences begin with a static *he was.* "His grip was dry and cool," however, adds a figurative element that sets one thinking: Could that handshake be captured in a simile? *More frail than I remembered*—I'm having a hard time keeping the camera on the subject rather than on myself. Finally, *cords* isn't right; it sounds young, even jaunty. Better return to *trousers.*

Final revision. The final version uses mostly active verbs (*hung, draped, shaking, clasping*), combines description and action, and shows more than tells the man's frailness. "Bird's claw" suggests the bony, dry, and cool images of the original version. There were other considerations in editing that brief passage, but they had to do with the *sound* of the words, a subject for Chapter 19.

Re-creating reality is the chief business of successful description, and re-creating reality depends upon presenting the right details. Any old detail won't do—nor will the most compelling detail if it does nothing to further theme and purpose. Irrelevant details or details that fight with each other are the wrong details. The right descriptive details generally have several things in common:

- They appeal to the senses. Strong, dramatic, suggestive description depends largely upon sensory writing.

- They're selected for impact, suggestiveness, and actual or symbolic meaning.
- They're organized and presented for coherence and point of view. The presentation of details can move from the general to the specific, for example, or from the specific to the general. The method of organization will be "invisible" to the casual reader, but its orderly and logical procession will still be felt.

Examine the organization of descriptive detail in the following passage. P.D. James' investigator Massingham has been led to this scene by a young boy, and James serves up the details to the reader as Massingham absorbs them. You can feel the investigator's roving eye at first zeroing in on the sleeping figure, then on the figure's surroundings. It's a smorgasbord of detail, but it isn't random. The author moves her camera from the specific to the general, much as any viewer would take in the scene, but no detail is irrelevant or haphazard. Is there nothing else to conjure up or remark in this setting—mauve wallpaper, velvet bedspread? Surely. But the details here serve the scene's purpose; whatever else may describe the setting would be beside the point.

She was lying on her back, naked except for a short wrapover dressing gown from which one blue-veined breast had escaped and lay like a quivering jellyfish against the pink satin. A thin line of lipstick outlined the moistly open mouth from which a bleb of mucus ballooned and fell. She was snoring gently, small guttural sounds as if there were phlegm in her throat. Her eyebrows had been plucked in the manner of the thirties, leaving thin arches high above the natural line of the brow. They gave the face, even in sleep, a look of clownish surprise, enhanced by the circles of rouge on both cheeks. On a chair beside the bed was a large jar of Vaseline, a single fly gummed to the rim. The back of the chair and the floor were strewn with clothes and the top of a chest of drawers which

served as a dressing table under an oval mirror was crowded
with bottles, dirty glasses, jars of make-up and packets of tis-
sue. Set incongruously amid the mess was a jam jar with a
bunch of freesias, still bound with a rubber band, whose deli-
cate sweetness was lost in the stink of sex, scent and whiskey.
    He said: 'Is this your ma?'

—P.D. James, *A Taste for Death*

That passage shows us that Massingham is appalled, not only through descriptive detail but also through Massingham's simple question—*Is this your ma?* The author does not have to tell us how Massingham feels.

In short, word pictures must be pertinent to the plot and move the action forward; they're there to say something, not just to adorn.

The great hazard with writers who learn to show instead of tell is that eventually they come to show too much, too often, and too long. This is particularly true of scene-setters—dreary and off-the-point blather about weather, place, wardrobe. In literature, the best picture is an action shot, not a static still life. Yet gratuitous scene setting is a favorite of writers who unnecessarily describe, writers for whom placing a character in a room becomes instead an exercise in interior decoration. It's a maddening habit, akin to conversation in which every anecdote is delayed by trivia—whether it occurred Tuesday or Wednesday or whether breakfast was pancakes or eggs or whether John was visiting, or Jane. If weather, place, or wardrobe *matters*, that's different. Likewise, a brief description of a character's physical appearance can help capture the character and can be both delightful and revealing. But those descriptions not only should add something to reader understanding, they also should be original, pertinent, and brief—not, as they so often are, long and labored and trite.

Jane was in what she called the "blue room"—a study
done entirely in French Provincial décor—when she heard that

had been senselessly, brutally slain. Sitting at her Louis
desk with John's last letter in her slender white fingers,
she wore a burgundy-colored velvet dressing gown that com-
plemented her hair, which was the color of cognac, or maybe
scotch, and which she still wore as long and straight as in her
Haight-Asbury days.

Yes, I made that up, but I've seen worse.

The classics are often filled with lavish description, of
course, and they are wonderful to read as classics, wonderful
for their day. But their day is not in the 21st century. The pen-
dulum swings in art and letters as it does in all things, and for
the moment, it has swung away from the overdone. While overwriting is seen as the fussy gewgaw of bad literature, however,
tight and telling description is not only welcome in good story
telling, it's vital.

A chief shortcut to those vital and tightly cropped word
pictures is figurative language—metaphor, simile, analogy, and
the like. We've seen some of those in this chapter: *An octave of*
good teeth. Lenses bristle like cannon barrels through open gun ports.
He looks at us as if he is about to throw his tin star in the dust. Eyeing
Jonathan through an imaginary gun slit. Eyes shallow as paint. Hands
like axheads. Present ourselves naked to the barbs of the world. One
blueveined breast lay like a quivering jellyfish.

Creating such delights is the business of the next chapter.

CHAPTER 18

Storytellers

Masters of Metaphor

By far the greatest thing is to be a master of metaphor. It is the one thing that cannot be learned from others. It is a sign of genius, for a good metaphor implies an intuitive perception of similarity among dissimilars.

—Aristotle

As we saw in the last chapter, good storytellers have a knack for making us see what they are saying whether their descriptions are literal or figurative. Certain images, however, stick in the mind like a burr. Long ago, I read somewhere—perhaps in a novel by Peter De Vries, but don't hold me to it—that a young woman had a mouth "like a jelly donut." I never forgot that image, which was another character's observation. The simile captured the red, juicy sweetness of that mouth—or at least the besotted admirer's perception of it.

Such is the power of good figurative language and its fresh imagery. You may forget author, work, and context, but you remember the image. Orphan similes and metaphors read or heard decades earlier lodge in our heads. They may be separated from their creators but they're adopted and loved just the same. Here are authorless images that have stuck like Velcro to my memory:

Springs to mind like toadstools after rain.
Eyes framed by the pleats of previous smiles.
An empty grin that flashed on and off like a neon sign.
Lay like an overweight body atop the city.
A half full moon, like a tipped bowl.
Hair that stuck up like hog bristles.
Silent as fish.

I remember people as thin as a wick, as plump as a partridge; people with marsupial cheeks, cheeks like a hamster's, like a bulldog's. I remember thyroid eyes, eyes pale as a wolf's, eyes set like raisins in the sagging pastry of the flesh. I remember many descriptions of a balding man's comb-over, but I remember best the combover resembling an EKG wave. I remember a man's tonsured head that was speckled like a thrush's egg. That an old woman wore a hat that looked as if it had been put through a wringer. That a man's dayold beard frosted his cheeks like sugared topping. That the air was thicker than soup, than chowder, that it hung like a damp sock. I remember that light streaming through cathedral windows stained the air.

While fresh images please, however, stale ones annoy. I once asked a friend about a novel on her desk: *Any good?* She sighed. "I'm sick of reading that a house's windows look like eyes." Of all she could have said about the book, she selected one stale simile and let it represent the whole work—warmed over, unoriginal, trite. Such is the effect of the stale image. Hack writers depend upon the hackneyed, while gifted writers are masters of metaphor and czars of simile. They treasure images, which to them are almost things—things to trade, to imitate, to borrow.

For example, I once described to *Dallas Morning News* reporter Doug Swanson, a superb writer of fiction as well as non-fiction, how an acquaintance's false lashes came unstuck at the corners and lay like caterpillars above her eyes. Some time later, he asked: *That caterpillar simile—is it yours, and if so, may I use it?* Flattered, I said of course. And when Swanson's next book, *96 Tears,* came out, there it was in the opening line: "She wore eyelashes that had been glued on, and they lay across her lids like furry black caterpillars."

Not only was my progeny onstage, but it also was in the company of the big-time fresh metaphor that Doug Swanson typically creates: The lass with the lashes also has a laugh that sounds as if it has been "hanging in a smokehouse next to a couple of country hams." Another Swanson character's hair "looks like roadkill." Yet another, a lowlife named Teddy— who, to quote James Thurber, is no dumber than an ox, but is no smarter either—is upset about a snag in his silk suit. When his companion makes light of it, Teddy chides: "You talk like silk grows on trees." Here's strong figurative expression from Swanson's novel *Big Town:* "Hal shot off a couple of rockets of laughter and showed Jack all his bridgework." "His hair looked combed with a claw hammer." "Flippo pulled his jacket aside like a matador's cape."

The broad umbrella of "figurative language" covers non-literal expression. "We *flew* across the lawn" is figurative. "We *ran* across the lawn" is literal. Novelist Elizabeth George created figurative expression when she wrote that the creases in a nattily dressed character's trousers looked as if they had been put there by "royal decree."

Metaphors and similes

Figures of speech come in various forms, but we're concerned here chiefly with metaphors and similes. A metaphor is a figure of speech that likens something to something else—it describes one thing in terms of another. Metaphor has broadened to the point where most dictionaries define it in part simply as "figurative language," but simile has remained narrow. The distinction between the terms is that a metaphor's comparison is implicit and a simile's is explicit, using the words "like" or "as." Consider, for example, this simile from sportswriter David Casstevens: "His voice sounds *like* a slow ride down a gravel road." If that were a metaphor: "His voice *was* a slow ride down a gravel road."

Metaphor and simile enrich expression because they deepen, amplify, and extend meaning. Through suggestion, they embroider the plain fabric of the literal. Notice that last sentence. It is metaphorical in its image of "embroidering" literal expression's "fabric"; there's no *real* embroidery and no *real* fabric. Metaphor and simile offer writers richer and more suggestive ways to express their ideas. But such images must be woven into the work; they shouldn't stick out *like a sore thumb* (that's a simile—and a stale one).

Shakespeare so excelled at figures of speech that 400 years later we routinely borrow his images, often without knowing it: *Who steals my purse steals trash. Cowards die many times before their deaths. Knit up the raveled sleeve of care. The ripest fruit falls first. Kill with kindness. Words laid on with a trowel. Elbow room. Naked truth. Salad days. Quiet as a lamb. Sink or swim. Pound of flesh. In my mind's eye.*

We all use metaphor and simile, even if not as sublime as Shakespeare's: *I laughed my head off. She cried her eyes out. That scared our pants off. He worked like a dog.* There's nothing literal about that language. Nor does it have to make sense. The body parts of those who laugh their heads off or cry their eyes out are present and accounted for—as are their pants. And dogs are notable for not working very hard at all. A friend described a party she'd attended by saying, first, that she'd *eaten herself into oblivion* and, second, that she'd *laughed herself into oblivion.* I waited in vain for a more believable assertion—that she'd *drunk herself into oblivion,* for example.

Figurative expression is by no means the chief province of fiction writers. Roger Angell, writing about baseball's Barry Bonds for *The New Yorker,* creates a clever simile: "Bonds—with his shortenedup black bat twitching behind his ear, and that short-arc slash at the ball ticking within—stands in the middle of the Giants' batting order *like an aneurysm.*"

The criteria for effective figurative language is not only freshness and originality, but also taste and appropriateness. Stale, strained, overdone, tasteless, or mixed metaphor fails—and sometimes spectacularly: *Thus does our ship of state steam down the river of no return, under full sail, engine sputtering, too few men at the oars.* You know you have trouble when readers pay more attention to metaphor than to message. The clichés "ship of state" and "river of no return" would already be too much, but then we wonder: Is it a ship, a steamboat, a sailboat, a motorboat, or a rowboat?

Mystery writer P.D. James excels at creating fresh metaphor and simile. In the following passage, from her novel *Devices and Desires*, she creates clothing that makes its wearer look "like a walking sofa" (simile):

> *A formidable female novelist, vigorously corseted in a florid cretonne two-piece which made her look like a walking sofa, had borne him off to pull out a crumple of parking tickets from her voluminous handbag and angrily demand what he was proposing to do about them.*

Notice that this character doesn't hand over a *bunch* or a *handful* of parking tickets—easier and less suggestive language—but a *crumple* of parking tickets (metaphor). Consider that telling little word *crumple*: She has carelessly thrust those tickets into her handbag and carried them with her awhile—not with the intent to pay them, but to vent her outrage at receiving them.

Here's more simile and metaphor from P.D. James:

> *Like a Russian doll, one deceit was unscrewed to find another nestling within it.*
>
> *She lay there, sleek and curved as a fish or a gull.*
>
> *She knew that she was over-defensive, probably she always would be. Those early years couldn't be wiped out and they couldn't be forgotten. But surely she could let down one small drawbridge without yielding the whole fortress.*

Author Pat Conroy dealt in metaphor when he wrote that you could add a little vinegar to a character's voice and "pour it on a Caesar salad." Or that "five o'clock sunlight divided her face into symmetrical slats." A Peter De Vries character attending a social gathering entered a room "swollen with hypocrisy" and another entered a room in which he had to cross "an archipelago of small rugs."

Analogy

Comparison and finding similarities is also the business of the analogy—one of the most dependable devices for making difficult, unfamiliar, or technical material interesting and easy to understand. Analogies relate the unfamiliar to the familiar. They often make connections between the abstract and the concrete, or between the complicated and the simple, by finding parallels in process, action, or function.

One might, for example, explain an unfamiliar process by likening it to a familiar process—the workings of a car engine, for example, or a human being's digestive process.

Analogies can be brief or extended. A newspaper story about a premature baby's struggle for life began with a brief analogy. It asked the reader to imagine holding a 16-oz. package of cheese in the palm of the hand. That writer emphasized—and helped the reader understand—how very small the preemie was by likening his weight to the same weight of something familiar.

Here's another brief analogy, from poet Robert Frost: "Talking is a hydrant in the yard and writing is a faucet upstairs in the house. Opening the first takes all the pressure off the second."

And another from film critic Philip Wuntch of *The Dallas Morning News*: "Waterworld. By now, the name conjures up images of a postmodern theme park where money flows like bilge water, stars declare mutiny, directors walk the plank and hungry critics circle like sharks."

The following is an extended analogy from *Dallas Morning News* writer Rick Holter:

A director making an action thriller is a lot like an assassin making a long-range hit. It's a delicate, methodical process, one that takes months of detailed planning, pinpoint control and just a dollop of insanity.

But even if the preparation is letter-perfect, it all comes down to the shooter's timing when the mark is in his sights. Pull the trigger too soon, before the scene settles out, and risk taking out an innocent bystander. Wait even a moment too long, and rock-steady hands start twitching, a droplet of sweat slips into an eye, a clean kill becomes a bloody mess.

With Assassins, director Richard Donner comes closer to a direct hit than he has in years. Yet his reluctance to finish the job with a quick shot to the heart causes unnecessary suffering.

Allusion

The literary devices above make connections through association. The allusion is another "connection" device. Although allusions function differently from metaphors, similes, and analogies, they too extend and enrich meaning through association. The allusion *alludes*. It refers to something else—a person, event, work of art or literature—something the reader will recognize and understand. The most effective allusions are those that can assume common knowledge. But if there's doubt, enough of the allusion can be explained so that the reader is not at sea.

For example, the opening pages of Elizabeth George's novel *Missing Joseph* brought me a pleasant and unexpected experience. George takes one of her characters to an exhibit of Leonardo da Vinci's Virgin and Child with St. Anne and St. John the Baptist. As the author described the work, my eyes flew to a picture on my own wall: She was describing the first work of art I'd ever bought, when I was barely out of my teens, one that has graced my walls these decades since. George's character gazed at Leonardo's work, noting what I've noted hundreds of times—the infant's plump hand reaching for the older child,

St. Anne's unfinished finger pointing skyward, the devotion on both women's faces:

> *For who would understand better than St. Anne, watching her own beloved daughter loving the wondrous Infant she'd borne. And the Infant Himself, leaning out of His mother's arms, reaching for His cousin the Baptist, leaving His mother even now, even now . . . .*

Elizabeth George's allusion brought me not only a sense of rediscovery but also one of shared experience. That's the power of allusion. This one had special meaning to me personally, but it would have been successful in any case because of George's description, which in turn suggested much of the book's theme.

Here's another allusion from Elizabeth George. This one, from *Deception on His Mind*, likens a stagnant community to Charles Dickens' famous Miss Haversham:

> *Years of isolation from the tourist trade—as inexpensive holiday packages to Spain became more alluring than a drive to Essex—had leeched the lifeblood from the local economy. The result lay before her like an urban Miss Haversham, jilted and frozen in a fragment of time.*

Allusions can entertain and amuse as well as deepen and enrich—especially if they employ surprise. Dan Akroyd and Harold Ramis, who wrote the screenplay for "Ghostbusters," alluded to Julius Caesar's celebrated "veni, vidi, vici" (I came, I saw, I conquered) with "We came, we saw, we kicked its ass." Another play on this particular allusion is "Veni, vidi, Visa" (we came, we saw, we shopped).

Foreshadowing
Foreshadowing is yet another storytelling device that capitalizes on making connections. It alludes to later events in a narrative and is a highly effective means of preparing the reader

for what is to come. Foreshadowing can be a simple allusion or hint of future developments: *You won't believe what happened next.* Or it can refer to an arrangement of events or details in a narrative—an arrangement that suggests a certain outcome. The latter sort of foreshadowing promotes unity of structure and theme because the end is built into the beginning.

In any case, foreshadowing can create interest, build suspense, and provoke curiosity. We dealt at length with the value of the unanswered question in chapters 15 and 16; it's enough to say here that foreshadowing is a principal tool for creating unanswered questions.

Effective foreshadowing can be found in any medium. Bette Davis uttered a famous foreshadowing line in the 1950 movie "All About Eve," a line penned by screenwriter Joseph Leo Mankiewicz: "Fasten your seatbelts. It's going to be a bumpy night." Equally famous is Humphrey Bogart's foreshadowing comment in the film "Casablanca": "Of all the gin joints in all the towns in all the world, she walks into mine!"

The late historian Stephen Ambrose foreshadows in his book *Undaunted Courage:* "It would take a month for Lewis's letter to reach Clark, another ten days for his reply to arrive. Meanwhile, a mystery." Ambrose's "meanwhile, a mystery" engages our interest and keeps us reading.

Joseph Conrad foreshadows in the opening paragraphs of the novel *Victory:*

> *At that epoch in his life, in the fullness of his physical development, of a broad, martial presence, with his bald head and long moustaches, he resembled the portraits of Charles XII of adventurous memory. However, there was no reason to think that Heyst was in any way a fighting man.*

The readers understand from "there was no reason to think that Heyst was in any way a fighting man," that we shall shortly find him fighting. Such devices add dimension not only to the action, but also to the characters.

Finally, here is foreshadowing from Ian McEwan's *Atonement*:

> *The search parties were setting off as he reached the front door . . . . He had already decided: if he could not be with Cecilia, if he could not have her to himself, then he too, like Briony, would go out searching alone. This decision, as he was to acknowledge many times, transformed his life.*

The pregnant words "that decision transformed his life" foreshadow the rest of the book's action. The words have a chill, and they create in the readers not only dread and suspense, but also a desire to keep reading.

Non-fiction writers tend to neglect foreshadowing, but it's perfectly appropriate for features, profiles, and the like. And the nice thing is it doesn't take special skill—foreshadowing is fairly easy to execute.

One caution: Audiences understand foreshadowing so well that they may suppose a random detail has meaning. Artists don't traffic in random details; everything in their work has a purpose. "One must not put a loaded rifle on the stage," said playwright Anton Chekhov, "if no one is thinking of firing it." That famous Chekhov remark is quoted more fully in S. Shchukin's *Memoirs*: "If you say in the first chapter that there is a rifle hanging on a wall, in the second or third chapter it absolutely must go off. If it's not going to be fired, it shouldn't be hanging there."

Irony

Unlike the devices above that capitalize on similarities, irony exploits contradiction and dissimilarities. Irony is essentially an incongruity between word and meaning, between appearance and reality, or between action and consequence. Almost any definition of irony short-changes it, however. Irony is a detached, subtle, oblique product of intellect. It can be angry, sardonic, amusing, or tragic. We appreciate the word more when we understand that one of its synonyms is *wit*—meaning, in this case, intellectual perception and perspective, the ability to see contradiction, paradox, and absurdity. Irony is one of the satirist's chief weapons.

Sadly, *irony* is a much misused and misunderstood word. Some writers use it without a single clue to its meaning. A sports commentator, for example, said that an athlete had signed to play for a New England team, which was ironic because he was born in New England. That may be a *coincidence* (and not a very big one at that), but it certainly is not ironic.

What is irony? It comes in several broad forms: verbal, situation, or dramatic. Verbal irony is using a word to suggest its opposite. A critic of using animals for medical research may identify such practice, for example, as "just one reflection of humankind's *superiority* over animals." That ironic statement intends the opposite: The practice of experimenting on animals suggests that humankind is *not* superior.

Verbal irony is not always that broad. In its subtlest forms, it attaches to ideas and not just to definitions. A statement in John Hersey's *Hiroshima* is brilliant in its subtle irony: "There, in the tin factory, in the first moment of the atomic age, a human being was crushed by books." The reader is likely to be struck by that sentence's imagery without identifying its irony, which is in the juxtaposition of low tech (tin) and high tech (atomic bomb) with where knowledge is stored (books). The readers understand, perhaps subliminally, that the man was crushed by the source as well as the result of learning.

Abraham Lincoln was an ironist. When he met Harriet Beecher Stowe, author of *Uncle Tom's Cabin,* he said: "So you're the little woman who started this great big war." The incongruity of a little woman and a great big war is verbal irony.

Situation irony, as you might guess, derives from situation rather than from words. A famous example of such irony is in Joseph Heller's novel *Catch-22:*

> *There was only one catch and that was Catch-22, which*
> *specified that a concern for one's own safety in the face of*

dangers that were real and immediate was the process of a rational mind. Orr was crazy and could be grounded. All he had to do was ask; and as soon as he did, he would no longer be crazy and would have to fly more missions . . . . If he flew them, he was crazy and didn't have to; but if he didn't want to he was sane and had to . . . .

'That's some catch, that Catch-22,' he [Yossarian] observed.

'It's the best there is,' Doc Daneeka agreed.

The stories of O. Henry (William Sidney Porter) are still frequently anthologized after a century and testify to the force of irony. One of his best-known tales, "The Gift of the Magi," concerns Jim and Della Young, who have no money to buy one another a Christmas gift. Yet each has one prized possession: "One was Jim's gold watch that had been his father's and his grandfather's. The other was Della's hair."

Della, determined to buy her husband something for Christmas, sells her hair to a hair goods shop and buys Jim a platinum fob chain for his cherished watch. Meanwhile, Jim also has been busy: He has sold his watch and bought a set of jeweled tortoise-shell combs Della had admired but never hoped to own. In this mutual sacrifice is situation irony: Each gives up something to buy a gift that requires that thing the other has given up.

I once witnessed a delicious irony when a pompous psychology professor was talking about the Freudian slip, a subject in which he considered himself especially adept. During his talk, he said: "We can count the number of experts in my field on *one finger.*" He did not recognize his own Freudian slip and was bewildered by the explosion of laughter from the audience.

Slapstick comedy sometimes uses situation irony. One player is laughing wildly at the pie on another's face, even as we see the pie headed for the laugher. The irony is in the *second* pie—and in the fact that we see it coming, but the player does not.

Dramatic irony usually shares that feature: We see what's coming, but the character cannot. In Herman Melville's *Moby Dick,* Ahab is obsessed by the white whale that took his leg. He is compelled to chase the whale, to seek vengeance. The readers want to say: *Oh, let it go, you can live with one leg, but seeking revenge may exact a greater price.* The readers see something that Ahab is blind to: Obsession can be a fatal flaw. So he goes to the deep, and to his death, strapped to the back of the white whale—strapped, in ironic terms, to the back of the obsession he let steal his life.

The wag who first said "Watch what you ask for; you might get it" was an ironist.

Effective irony will enrich your work whether you're writing essays, editorials, fiction, or nonfiction. It's among the deepest, most enriching, and most meaningful literary or rhetorical devices. It's also among the most difficult. That's because irony requires not only creativity and craft, but also vision and wisdom.

Word play

After a long walk, a clever friend said her feet were on their last legs. Peter De Vries wrote of a character whose heavy chest cold gave a whole new meaning to the term "infectious laugh." When actress Jean Harlow called Margot Asquith "Lady Margott," the latter said: "My dear, the T in my name is silent, as in *Harlow*." Here are other word players at work:

Saul Bellow: "She was what we used to call a suicide blonde—dyed by her own hand."

David Chambless: "Better to have loved and lost a short person than never to have loved a tall."

Joe E. Lewis: "I always wake up at the crack of ice."

Word play takes its proper place among effective and attention-getting linguistic devices. Unlike the other devices in this chapter, word play has little serious intent. Usually, it's just for fun—that's why it's called *play*. That it's play doesn't demean it, however—good word play takes considerable skill and imagination.

We find plays on words in every kind of writing and speaking. As with other linguistic devices, the only truly pleasing word play is fresh and original—that's because its success depends largely upon surprise, and we're surprised only by what is new to us.

Word play has many forms. It can use words in unexpected or contradictory ways. It can employ wry under- or over-statement. It can involve wit or a pun—using a word that has two or more senses in a comic way. There's even a special kind of pun called a *zeugma*, which involves one verb and more than one object, one of which is unanticipated: *She tossed back her cloak, her hair, and a jigger of whiskey. When he saw her standing in the rain, he opened his umbrella and his heart.*

Some writers of factual material think word play is too informal for their purposes. But clever word play is welcome wherever it's appropriate to vehicle and subject, and it also can relieve the dullness of a "just the facts, ma'am" approach. *The Dallas Morning News'* Al Brumley wrote in a story regarding arts groups waiting for NEA funding: "The waiting is the hardest art." A *Washington Times* reporter, David Sands, wrote in a story about Agriculture committee problems: "Out in the back 40, they're stuck on square 1." Richard Schickel wrote in a *Time* film review: "His re-creations of their famously brittle conversations suffer from a desperate case of fallen archness." And Lisa Fine, writing for the Durham, N.C., *Herald-Sun*, wrote in a story on an animal fashion show: "The bride batted her puppy-dog brown eyes from beneath a delicate lace veil. The groom wore a top hat and tails, one of which he wagged."

Those examples show that some writers are limited by lack of imagination rather than by the unsuitability of figurative expression or literary device.

CHAPTER 19

Storytelling

Let Sound Echo Sense

> *Touched by poetry, language is more fully language.*
> —Octavio Paz

One of the most unattractive families in literature is William Faulkner's large and repellent Snopes family, whose members appear throughout Faulkner's fiction. The family, led by patriarch (or anti-patriarch, as some would have it) Abner Snopes, comprises an assemblage of bad actors—among them are swindlers, arsonists, thieves, murderers, and bigamists. Faulkner gave the Snopeses such various and ugly names as Flem, Eck, Mink, or Lump.

Faulkner obviously created the Snopeses with care, and in using a name beginning with the letters SN, he *named* them with care as well. He wanted a name that *sounded* as bad as the people.

Words make more than meaning; they make sounds, and Faulkner knew that SN words often identified something distasteful or unpleasant: *snot, snake, snarl, snivel, snob, sneak, snide, snub, snitch, snit, sneer, snoop, snaggletooth*, and so forth. He was persnickety about the words he chose, as careful writers are, because he knew he could get more mileage out of words that had the right sound.

Consider the words "ghostly galleon," from Alfred Noyes' poem "The Highwayman." Say it aloud: *ghostly galleon*. Now try "phantom-like galleon." Or "spooky galleon." Or *incorporeal, unworldly, ethereal, intangible, wraith-* or *specter-like* galleon. Those choices show that Noyes used the appropriate word for his context. He used, as Mark Twain admonished, "the right word, not its second cousin."

Words don't just happen. People think them up. And often they think them up because they're somehow suggestive of what they define. They may even be onomatopoeic—that is, they make the sound they define: *buzz, hiss, pop, moo, whoosh, zoom.*

Important as it is, sound is one of the most neglected aspects of our writing education. We may go through our entire schooling, university education included, without learning about the effect of how words sound. Or we may get "sound" training in a poetry class, but it's not guaranteed even there.

Some words are inherently beautiful, some ugly. Some are silken or rough. Some words are harsh or guttural; some are staccato or herky jerky. Some words mesh well together, some don't. Those effects are determined by the sound the words make. And there's no shortage of choice in the English language, which has catalogued more than 600,000 words.

Informational or factual writers usually attend little to sound, yet it matters in all writing, not just in creative work. Sounds that work well together help the writing to move along smoothly; sounds that don't work well together roughen the work and hinder the reader's progress. Words have a music of their own, and the best music supports or reinforces meaning— that is, the sound echoes the sense.

Alexander Pope offers his poetic opinion on the subject:

> *True ease in writing comes from art, not chance.*
> *As those move easiest who have learn'd to dance.*
> *'Tis not enough no harshness gives offense;*
> *The sound must seem an echo to the sense.*

How do we make the sound echo the sense? The means is well demonstrated in the final sentences of Chief Joseph's speech to the Nez Percé tribe after the 1877 battle of Bear Paw Mountains—a speech we looked at in detail in Chapter 3: "My heart is sick and sad. From where the sun now stands, I will fight no more forever." The sound of Chief Joseph's words reinforce his sense; they are rich in sibilant S's, resonant N's, M's, L's, and R's, and softly aspirant F's.

My heart is sick and sad.
From where the sun now stands,
I will fight no more forever.

The soft, shushing S, Z, and soft C can be meditative or melancholy, depending upon the context. And N's, M's, L's, and R's can purr, whine, or moan, again depending on context. Soft aspirants can have the same effects, depending upon context. In short, there's nothing hard, harsh, or aggressive here; the sound of Chief Joseph's words is the sound of defeat. And that sound, coupled with the simplicity and dignity of his message, makes unforgettable poetry.

The brief catalog below discusses the major sounds and how they work:

Euphony is a general term meaning pleasant, melodic, or flowing sounds. Long vowels often yield euphony; so do liquid consonants such as S or certain soft aspirants.

Rhyme. In prose, rhyme is pleasing, amusing, or annoying depending upon whether it's deliberate, accidental, or appropriate. Deliberate rhyme in prose is amusing if the subject matter is lighthearted. Accidental rhyme seems careless, the product of a writer with a tin ear. In serious or grave material, rhyming word play in general seems inappropriate and at least undignified, if not repellent.

Rewriting a passage that appears elsewhere in this book (Chapter 21, "Speedbumps"), I tried: "Technology may have freed us from conventional war, which in the past consumed the whole nation and annihilated an entire generation." You'll see immediately what's wrong with that sentence: the unwitting rhyme of *nation* and *generation*. Deliberate rhyme for special effects can be pleasant; unwitting rhyme almost never is. Here, the rhyme sets up an unintended poetic cadence—either *nation* or *generation* had to go. *Nation* was easier, and the rewrite finally read: "Technology may have freed us from conventional war, which in the past consumed the whole country and annihilated an entire generation." Not only did the unhappy rhyme disappear, but the new version also delivered a sound effect bonus: *Country* echoes the hard C in *technology* and alliterates with *conventional* and *consumed*.

Internal rhyme occurs when words within a line rhyme— whether or not there is rhyme at line's end. Prose can contain pleasing internal rhyme, but it quickly becomes too much if readers start noticing the device. Internal rhyme combined with end-of-line rhyme, as often seen in song lyrics, yields catchy rhythms that are easy to remember and fun to imitate. W.S. Gilbert's "Patience" libretto shows how entertaining internal rhyme can be: "Though the Philistine may jostle, you will rank as an apostle in the high aesthetic band / If you walk down Piccadilly with a poppy or a lily in your medieval hand."

Alliteration is the repetition of sound, as a consonant or cluster, at the beginning of words or stressed syllables—for example, *Peter Piper picked, part and parcel, stem to stern, wild and woolly*. Alliteration is common in nonsense verse, tongue-twisters, and jingles. It's catchy, easy to create, and easy to remember—witness a famous radio message to a U.S. Navy Base in 1942: "Sighted sub, sank same."

Like rhyme, alliteration can be amusing or annoying, even ludicrous, depending upon context and intent. Former vice president Spiro Agnew knew about the staying power of alliteration; he damned the press with the still-quoted "nattering nabobs of negativism." In Alan Jay Lerner's 1956 production of "My Fair Lady," actor Rex Harrison, as Henry Higgins (itself alliterative), offers a good example of alliteration: "In Hertford, Hereford, and Hampshire, hurricanes hardly happen." And in the film "The Court Jester," comedian Danny Kaye amusingly mixes alliteration and internal rhyme: "The pellet with the poison's in the flagon with the dragon, the vessel with the pestle has the brew that is true."

Sibilance comes from whispering, hissing, or liquid consonant sounds: S, SH, Z, ZH, soft C, CH (when it sounds like *tsh*) and J (when it sounds like *dzh*). The following sibilant lines (from which Marcel Proust famously borrowed) are from Shakespeare's Sonnet 30: "When to the sessions of sweet silent thought / I summon up remembrance of things past."

Resonance is a continuing sound—a vibration in, for example, the mouth or nasal chambers. In voiced sounds, resonance comes from letters you can "hold": N, NG, M, L, R, Y, W, etc. "A low stone wall strewn with green vines ran the length of the maison" is a resonant passage. Read it aloud to hear the sounds resonate.

Consonance is easy to remember because it sounds like what it concerns: *consonants.* Consonance in voiced sounds is the repetition of consonant sounds, especially at the end of stressed syllables: *march, lurch; stick, stuck; stroke, luck.* "A frog's croak mixed with the creak of timbers" has consonance.

Assonance comes from the repetition and juxtaposition of similar sounds, especially of vowels. Sometimes called "vocalic rhyme," assonance differs from rhyme in that the consonant sounds usually aren't repeated—*hazy* and *crazy* create rhyme, for example, while *bony* and *holy, old* and *oak,* and *keep* and *reel* create assonance. The long A's of *the rain in Spain stays mainly in the plain,* from "My Fair Lady," is a good example of assonance as well as resonance. So is Peter De Vries' "From the radio came the strains of 'Charmaine.'"

Onomatopoeia is seen in a word that imitates the sound associated with that word, or that suggests the word's sense: *whir, crackle, staccato.* In *A Small Town in Germany,* John LeCarré uses the onomatopoeic word *juddered* to describe the unpleasant thing windshield wipers do when the glass is too dry for the wipers to run smoothly: "The engine was still running, shaking the car with inner pains. A wiper juddered uselessly over the grimy windshield."

Cacophony is dissonance or harshness in sound—the opposite of euphony. Hard C or K sounds and other harsh or guttural letters, such as hard G, often contribute to cacophony, which can be unpleasant or purposeful to create a special effect.

Hard C and K sounds are high energy and staccato sounds and usually command a certain attention. Here's a hard C or K sentence from Peter De Vries: "He sucked the cold pipe between bright teeth and pulled from it an occasional death rattle." F. Scott Fitzgerald's *The Great Gatsby* alliterates a hard C in: "A corps of caterers came down with several hundred feet of canvas and enough colored lights to make a Christmas tree." And Alfred, Lord Tennyson's "Morte D'Arthur" offers a cacophonous passage:

> *Dry clashed his harness in the icy caves*
> *And barren chasms, and all to left and right*
> *The bare black cliff clanged round him, as he based*
> *His feet on juts of slippery crag . . . .*

It's easy to think that special sound effects are reserved for creative efforts—for fiction or poetry—but in the passage below, reporter Brad Bailey, writing for *The Dallas Morning News*, uses K and hard C words to make sound echo sense:

> *It's the kind of bar where they sell pickled pigs' feet out of a jar, and hard-boiled eggs, and pork hocks and Fat Freddie Summer Sausage, the kind of place decorated in cheap mirror-tile, low light, and wall calendars.*
>
> *It's a hard bar on a rough street, and it's full of hardscrabble survivors.*
>
> *But it's not the kind of bar where a guy you thought you knew would bring in an M-16 and open fire, shattering the mirrors, pocking the paneling, and killing his friends.*

That passage is subtly onomatopoeic in that Bailey imitates the hard, repetitive staccato of fire from an M-16. Look at the harsh and harsh-sounding words he chooses—the emphasis on words such as *hard, rough,* or *hardscrabble* and the high-energy hard C and K sound:

"It's the <u>k</u>ind of bar where they sell pi<u>ck</u>led pigs' feet out of a jar, and <u>hard</u>-boiled eggs, and por<u>k</u> ho<u>ck</u>s . . . the <u>k</u>ind of place de<u>c</u>orated in cheap mirror-tile, low light, and wall <u>c</u>alendars. It's a <u>hard</u> bar on a <u>rough</u> street, and it's full of <u>hardscrabble</u> survivors. But it's not the <u>k</u>ind of bar where a guy you thought you knew would bring in an M-16 and open fire, shattering the mirrors, po<u>ck</u>ing the paneling, and <u>k</u>illing his friends."

This catalog of sound does not exhaust the subject, but it comprises the usual concerns. Knowing which sounds create which effects helps writers craft more effective work. Sometimes writers are not trying to support or echo a mood as much as they're simply trying to get the best and most meaningful mesh of sounds. In our discussion on description (Chapter 17), we considered my successive editing of the following passage: "He was more frail than I remembered— baggy gray trousers hung on his hipbones, and an old black cardigan loosely draped his hollow chest. Shaking his hand was like clasping a bird's claw."

Beyond description, my considerations also had to do with the *sound* of the words. Working on the simile "like clasping a bird's claw," I first wrote that *"clasping* his hand was like *grasping* a bird's claw"—an awful moment of unwitting rhyme. Then, "like *shaking* a bird's claw." Not right. Then, "like *seizing* a bird's claw." Even worse. Yet the S on *seizing* melded nicely with the S's in *shaking, was,* and *bird's. Clasping* was perfect in both sound and sense—it not only had that attractive S, but also a hard C that alliterated with *claw* and *cardigan* as well as the K's in *shaking* and *like.*

We could extract many lessons in sound from the following passage, which appears in Charles Dickens' *A Christmas Carol* and which we already discussed in Chapter 1. The passage mixes sibilance, resonance, and assonance with high-energy sounds for maximum effect.

> *Oh, but he was a tightfisted hand at the grindstone.*
> *Scrooge! a squeezing, wrenching, grasping, scraping, clutch-*
> *ing, covetous old sinner! Hard and sharp as flint, from which*
> *no steel had ever struck out generous fire; secret, and self-*
> *contained, and solitary as an oyster.*

You cannot separate sound from poetry, and the elements of poetry can be found in the prose of good writers whatever they write. This is true whether or not those writers consciously consider such things as meter, rhythm, or the play of one word against another. That's because the language moves as it should in the hands of those who understand it—even if on a visceral rather than intellectual level.

In a newsroom, where people are often more concerned with information than with music, you don't expect to see newswriters monitoring the sound—counting the number of metrical feet in a line or checking stresses, trochees, or iambs. Yet we find poetry where we least expect it. Newswriters—especially feature writers, since they have more latitude for creativity—frequently write poetic prose. Sometimes their work is so balanced and melodic that you can extract little poems from its clauses. Consider this passage from theater critic Jeremy Gerard, writing for *The Dallas Morning News*:

> *Marianne Owen projects so easy a grace on stage that the*
> *setting she inhabits becomes a living room, each word spoken*
> *an intimacy shared. Watch her cross the stage of the Plaza*
> *Theatre, a tough kid with a bad leg and a dance of light in the*
> *pale almond eyes that stare at you—for you are the only per-*
> *son in the theater—straight on. Even with her hair tied back*
> *in a careless knot and a plain sack of a dress hanging from her*
> *shoulders, you can't ignore the elegant welcoming that draws*
> *you into her world.*

A small poem emerges from the sound and mesh of those words:

Each word spoken
An intimacy shared
A tough kid with a bad leg
And a dance of light
In the pale almond eyes
You can't ignore
The elegant welcoming
That draws you into her world

Diction and meter often create poetic prose. And the following passage by sports writer Dan Barreiro for *The Dallas Morning News* demonstrates another important device—repetition: "When all was wrong with Jay Vincent, when his game had abandoned him, and his coach has lost respect for him, and his mother had prayed for him, all he wanted to do was sleep."

That sentence shows how meter and stylistic repetition can help move a passage along. Parallel structure plays an important role as well. Perfectly balanced and repeated parallel structures yield a stately sort of poetry. We see such balance in the King James Version of the Holy Bible, throughout Shakespeare, and in the works of such poets as, say, Walt Whitman. Here is an example of such diction:

God reprimanding Job: *Where was thou when I laid the foundations of the earth . . . Hast thou given the horse strength . . . Hast thou clothed his neck with thunder . . . Doth the hawk fly by thy wisdom . . . Doth the eagle mount up at thy command?*

Whitman: *The spotted hawk swoops by and accuses me, he complains of my gab and my loitering. I too am not a bit tamed, I too am untranslatable, I sound my barbaric yawp over the roofs of the world.*

Could such heavy rhythms be adopted for everyday informational writing? Below, Christine Wicker, writing for *The*

Dallas Morning News, achieves a humorous effect by applying stately balance and dramatic repetition—usually reserved for grave and weighty matter—to the trivial:

> *It was get fit or get fat. We knew the rules of God and mammon. We had seen the long-legged women with their three-inch heels and narrow hips. We had seen the flat-stomached men rippling their muscles under their Izod shirts. We too wanted youth and beauty. We too wanted pride and wealth. We too wanted to be lean and mean—but not hungry. We wanted the solace of icy margaritas and sizzling fajitas. The gourmet grocers beckoned, the French bakers called out to us, the Jewish delis spoke to us of delights we thought only New Yorkers could have. Our workdays were long. Our automobiles awaited, ready to glide us to new discos where we could dance and drink late into the night. Our friends clamored for attention and parties waned without our presence. Could we have it all?*

Richard Wright capitalizes on repetition, parallel structure, and a staccato cadence of short successive sentences to make a point in *Native Son*: "Godammit, look! We live here and they live there. We black and they white. They got things and we ain't. They do things and we can't. It's just like living in jail."

The examples above show that sentences as well as words have sounds—cumulative cadences and rhythms that further or foil the writer's intent. Here's a sentence from a James Lee Burke story, "We Build Churches, Inc.," which appears in *The Convict, and Other Stories:*

> *Then the winter swept down out of China across the Yalu, and the hills cracked clear and sharp, and our F-80s and B-25s bombed them twelve hours a day with napalm and phosphorous and incendiaries that generated so much heat in the soil that the barren slopes were still smoking the next morning.*

Compare the sound of that sentence with this:

> *Winter swept out of China across the Yalu, and the hills cracked clear and sharp. Our F-80s and B-25s bombed them twelve hours a day. We used napalm, phosphorous, and incendiaries . . . .*

There's nothing wrong with the second version, but something is lost. What is that something? What does James Lee Burke accomplish with the run-on sound and feel of the first sentence? Consider it again: "*Then* the winter swept down out of China across the Yalu, *and* the hills cracked clear and sharp, *and* our F-80s and B-25s bombed them twelve hours a day with napalm *and* phosphorous *and* incendiaries . . . ."

The device of the run-on helps show instead of tell. It helps the reader understand what Burke doesn't want to spell out: *The bombing was ceaseless; just went on and on and on . . . like this sentence.*

Now listen to that word *barren*. Why is it there, before "slopes"? The passage would be silkier without it: "so much heat in the soil that the slopes were still smoking the next morning." But Burke has a concern here beyond silken flow. *Barren* slows the passage a bit; it's a lonely and deliberate sound among all those sibilant S's. And it has a job: It emphasizes the awful heat of the bombing. The hills were bare—that smoke didn't come from burning trees and brush because there was nothing there to burn; *barren* makes it clear that all that heat came from bombs.

Again, sentences and words don't just happen in the work of good writers, even if they don't analyze their choices. Good writers speed the sentence here, slow it there, in the same way that good painters "choose" that swatch of red or black—through artistic instinct. The measure of genius is often found in a canny ability to make the right choices.

"Every fine story," writes Willa Cather, "must leave in the mind of the sensitive reader an intangible residuum of pleasure, a cadence, a quality of voice that is exclusively the writer's own, individual, unique." Obviously, effective writing cannot be achieved by sound or poetic device alone. Rhyme, rhythm, and song are wonderful as far as they go. But they go nowhere unless we also have something worth saying.

And we must be careful. A too-neat beat, an unfortunate rhythm, an excess of repetition or alliteration, can make the work ridiculous. The work of good writers, however, assures us that once we've satisfied the basic demands of accuracy, clarity, and brevity in our prose, a little poetry can't hurt.

CHAPTER 20

Pace

Write Fast, Edit Slow

Never fear or despise the public. Coax it, charm it, interest it, stimulate it, shock it now and then if you must, make it laugh, make it cry, but above all, never, never, never bore the hell out of it.
—Noel Coward

I remembered Noel Coward's counsel when I saw the 1971 film version of Thomas Mann's novella "Death in Venice." A friend and I watched interminable shots of Dirk Bogarde, the star, doing nothing. We studied him as he studied the world, viewed the panorama he viewed, and in no time at all, the movie was boring the eyeballs right out of our heads. And at the same moment, we turned to each other and exclaimed passionately: *My god but this is slow!*

Those who love the arts can put up with a lot, apparently, but the thing even the most charitable audience cannot tolerate is boredom. We finally cannot forgive *slow*. That's because *fast* is interesting and *slow* is dull. *Slow* puts us on tenterhooks. *Slow* makes us wait forever for the next word, next action, next scene—waiting, as it were, for the *first* shoe to drop.

If that's the case with cinema or theater, it's even more the case with writing, a narrow medium with a solitary audience and no distractions of color, light, or sound.

173

What is slow in print? Whatever is not fast. (See Chapter 22 for a fuller discussion of fast reading.) How can we tell what is fast? In part, by reading the work aloud. Reading aloud forces us to *listen*, and listening locates the hitches—bumps on the road that make a rough ride. Whatever interferes with the reader's progress and, thus, with the writer's message is an impediment to speedy and seamless flow. We can think of such impediments as *speedbumps*—and while actual speedbumps on actual streets usually have a positive result, speedbumps in writing never do.

What might constitute a speedbump? Errors in content or form. Distractions such as awkward phrasing. The wrong word. Dense, wordy, fuzzy, repetitive, tentative, or extraneous passages. Any "hitch" that reading aloud helps us find: Here we run out of breath; there the tongue balks; here a misplaced or inappropriate word rankles. Speaking and listening is vital—albeit neglected—to effective writing and editing. Our ear monitors what the eye may overlook: *sound*—the subject of the last chapter. I couldn't tell you how many times writers have asked me to listen to something they'd written and then, reading it, immediately began correcting it. *Well, that's not exactly the right word,* they might say, or *this part is kind of clumsy,* or *I guess that sentence isn't clear* . . . . Yet, until they *heard* the work, they were satisfied—satisfied enough to want to share it.

The late Stephen Ambrose, a historian and best-selling author of more than 20 books who is known for his readable prose, writes in his memoir *To America* that the secret of being a successful writer is to marry an English major. He writes of his wife:

> *Moira . . . has taught English in high school, is extremely well read, has a marvelous memory, and is never afraid to speak up. At the end of each day of writing, for the past four decades, I've read aloud to her whatever I've written that day.*

Obviously, in order to read your work aloud, you have to write it first—reading it aloud is actually part of the editing process. But what about the writing process? Is there an approach that will help you write fast-moving prose while you're still in the rough draft stage?

There is. I've heard this preparation referred to as "prewriting," but that's meaningless jargon. You're either writing or you're doing something else—thinking, researching, making and sorting notes. Those latter tasks are what you do before you write. And the better you do them, the faster, easier, and better the writing will be.

Here are half a dozen steps that smooth the way:

- If your task is informational writing, get all your information together before you begin writing.
- Find your exact focus or theme by reducing the main point of the whole project to one sentence. Identify the string that ties everything together.
- Break long projects into manageable pieces—chapters if a book, sections if a long story or report—and work on one at a time until it's finished.
- Devise beginning, middle, and end so you know where you're going.
- Using only elements that fit your focus, make a loose outline. Get the rest of your stuff out of your hair by storing it in a "maybe" folder, whether actual or electronic. You might want to color-key your notes with a handful of colored markers. Say your piece has three major parts or ideas—assign a different color to each section or idea: pink for section I, green for section II, blue for section III. That way you can group your notes with a glance rather than painstaking re-reading. Also, if a "pink" note has a misplaced passage, you can mark the wayward passage with its proper color and find it easily later.
- If your project involves sources, interviews, quotations, etc., keep those in one place, in a complete and updated "contact" list.

All those steps are chiefly to keep you from drowning in a sea of notes. Get a system that works for you. Whatever you're writing, chances are you'll have much more material than you'll ever use. You don't want that material to shove you around, but you do want to know exactly what you have and where to find it. Different writers devise different systems. Many use neatly typed or written note cards and an orderly filing system. That's too fussy for me; I'd fool with my note cards forever and never get to the writing.

The computer simplifies keeping track of material. My own system: clearly labeled folders that hold *everything*, including *maybe*; computer hard disk files that hold *probably*; computer desktop files that hold *absolutely*; and large 3-ring binders that hold *finished*. If I'm working on something long, I do a chapter or section at a time, not necessarily in sequence (I leave for last something I'm looking forward to working on). The whole process involves generating a lot of long-hand notes, making a brief, loose outline, typing a rough draft into the computer, and seeing it through three or four edits. When the chapter or section is as good as I can make it, I print it and put it in a big notebook decisively labeled: *Done*.

Ahhh.

For fast reading, the writing part of the process means—not surprisingly—fast *writing*. Most serious pace problems come from lack of focus and direction; the writer meanders, tempted by distracting possibilities. Knowing your destination and having a roadmap before you set out gets you there faster because you ignore the alternate routes. That's why, before laying hand to keyboard, you write a sentence that captures the essence of the whole piece or section or chapter. You can think of it as a thesis statement. Or you can write a headline, as long a headline as you like. The purpose of either is the same—to refine your message into one nugget of pure meaning. That meaning is your destination. Then you make a brief, informal outline that includes beginning, middle, and end. That's your roadmap.

Michelangelo said that when he received a new chunk of marble, he studied it until he saw a shape in it. Then he cut away everything that didn't belong to the shape. That's the sculptor's equivalent of focus, of getting to the point. Michelangelo didn't have to worry about being seduced or interrupted by myriad possibilities—since he already knew the shape, he also knew his main elements of form and design.

Stephen King's *On Writing* restates Michelangelo's protocol when King recalls working as a high school stringer for the local newspaper, where his first story was edited by one John Gould: "I took my fair share of English Lit classes in my two remaining years at Lisbon," King writes, "and my fair share of composition, fiction, and poetry classes in college, but John Gould taught me more than any of them, and in no more than ten minutes . . . ."

King recreates some of his story and Gould's editing:

'Last night, in the ~~well-loved~~ gymnasium of Lisbon High School, partisans and Jay Hills fans alike were stunned by an athletic performance unequaled in school history. Bob Ransom, ~~known as 'Bullet' Bob for both his size and accuracy,~~ scored thirty-seven points. Yes, you heard me right. Plus he did it with grace, speed . . . and with an odd courtesy as well, committing only two personal fouls in his ~~knight-like~~ quest for a record which has eluded Lisbon ~~thinclads since the years of Korea.~~'

Gould stopped at 'the years of Korea' and looked up at me. 'What year was the last record made?' he asked.

Luckily, I had my notes. '1953,' I said. Gould grunted and went back to work. When he finished marking my copy in the manner indicated above, he looked up and saw something on my face. I think he must have mistaken it for horror. It wasn't; it was pure revelation. Why, I wondered, didn't English teachers ever do this? . . .

'I only took out the bad parts, you know,' Gould said. 'Most of it's pretty good.'

'I know,' I said, meaning both things: yes, most of it was good—okay anyway, serviceable—and yes, he had only taken out the bad parts. 'I won't do it again.'

He laughed. 'If that's true, you'll never have to work for a living. You can do this instead. Do I have to explain any of these marks?'

'No,' I said.

'When you write a story, you're telling yourself the story,' he said. 'When you rewrite, your main job is taking out all the things that are not the story.'

One of the best ways of "taking out all the things that are not the story" is to try to keep them out of the story in the first place. (See chapters 15 and 16 for more on leaving things out.) That's where writing fast comes in. Once you have a clear focus, destination, and beginning, middle, and end, tell yourself the story: Sit down and write like mad, allowing no distraction, answering no phone, checking no fact. Fast writing helps keep story, voice, and flow intact while keeping extraneous material out. You can talk on the phone or check your facts later; both will still be there. But spontaneity is more fragile, and right now, you're *writing*.

Author Anne Lamott once said in a radio interview that there was a time when she couldn't write if there were dishes in the sink, but she had learned to shut out distractions, and now she could write if there were a *corpse* in the sink.

That's focus.

Stifle the impulse to edit as you write. You'll lose momentum if you do. Can't think of the right word? Use the almost right word—or just a couple of X's—and move on. Not sure of a fact? Check it later. Suspicious of this structure or grammar or punctuation? Mark it for later consideration and leave it. In short, you want to give full rein to your inner artist, to your creative right brain. Save rules and details for the editing process—give that left brain, which is so good at such mechanics, something to do. While editing, you can slow down and take your time. That's because, unfortunately, writing problems won't disappear as inspiration and spontaneity do—they're there to stay. So, pressure's off. Put on your mechanic's hat: You're going to edit. You'll fill the holes and solve the problems you ignored as you wrote in a fervor. You'll mercilessly cut away whatever doesn't belong—the gratuitous, tangential, or overblown—no matter how much you love it. You'll kill the babies, as some writing gurus call it.

But what you're really doing is leveling the speedbumps.

CHAPTER 21

Pace

Speedbumps

Nothing happens until something moves.

—Albert Einstein

As we discussed in the last chapter, any number of writing flaws can lead to slow reading. *Mistakes* are surefire speedbumps—little hurdles that impede flow because they stop the reader, if only for a moment. Other common speedbumps are failing to get to the point or to organize and present material logically, excessive length, obtrusive or tangential material, using the wrong word, and packing too much into sentences.

The worst place to find speedbumps is at the beginning of the trip. Slow starts lose many readers, and clumsily executed anecdotal beginnings are among the worst offenders. To succeed, anecdotal beginnings should be brief and pertinent and open an avenue into the story. Take the anecdote that opens the preceding chapter (an anecdote regarding a film version of Thomas Mann's novella "Death in Venice"). I used that anecdote because I thought it relevant and short enough (one paragraph) to lead us quickly to the third paragraph and the chapter's main point—that even the most charitable audience cannot tolerate boredom. The anecdote itself recounted an experience in tedium and therefore made a swift and easy bridge to that assertion.

Here, from a newspaper story, is a slow anecdotal beginning that shows the resulting muddle of not getting things moving right away.

A woman who fainted at a Meadowbrook bus stop awoke with no idea who she was. Doctors diagnosed amnesia. Police searched missing-person reports, publicized her plight in the media and even tried hypnosis using truth serum.

Five months later, a relative identified her from an episode of 'Unsolved Mysteries' as Jane Jones of San Francisco. The woman found her family—and an arrest warrant for theft back home.

Some doubted her story, saying she made it up to escape the law. But a psychology expert who worked on the 1992 case said recently that she may have had a rare psychiatric disorder in which people cannot face their past.

There's no way to prove whether someone has the disorder, according to experts. 'There's always that question: Are they faking it?' said Dr. John Johnson, a Meadowbrook psychologist.

That's the question members of the Meadowbrook Community Church are asking as they . . . .

At this point, the story launches into yet another long and detailed anecdote involving one Rev. Sam Stevens, a pastor who disappeared and said when recognized 17 years later that he had lost his memory.

This leisurely rendering of anecdotes is confusing. Readers first suppose that the story is about the woman who fainted at the bus stop. Then they must reorient themselves to suppose that the story is about the pastor. In fact, it is about neither. It is about a form of amnesia called "dissociative fugue" and the difficulty of diagnosing and verifying the disorder. The audience would be better served if that focus were immediately clear.

How could we keep this writer's anecdotal approach but speed things up so we present the story's purpose earlier? By cutting whatever isn't necessary to the story's form. The story is *not* the woman, and it's *not* the pastor. Those are just supporting anecdotes, and we signal that to the reader by telescoping them, by capturing essence, not detail:

> *Consider the woman who fainted at a Meadowbrook bus stop in 1992 and awoke with amnesia. Police searched missing-person records, publicized her plight, tried hypnosis and truth serum. Eventually, her identity was discovered—and so was a warrant for her arrest.*
>
> *Or take Sam Stevens, pastor of Meadowbrook Community Church, recognized in December as a man who'd disappeared from Baltimore in 1984. Stevens says he was found beaten and without memory in a small Tennessee town, a story police can't verify.*
>
> *Amnesia? Scam? Or 'dissociative fugue'?*
>
> *Psychologists say dissociative fugue is a rare disorder that causes people to 'blank out and start wandering' during psychological trauma. Dr. John Johnson, a Meadowbrook psychologist, said the mind has an amazing ability to block out unwelcome thought: 'A particular thread unites people in fugue states—they get into an impossible situation.'*
>
> *But, he added, there's always that question: 'Are they faking it?'*
>
> *At least a dozen people in the United States have faced intense public scrutiny in the last decade after they said amnesia had . . . .*

Through compression, the revision manages to say much more in less space. Both anecdotes are presented briefly in two short paragraphs, and the story's focus is clear by the third. The "dissociative fugue" material and the psychologist's words in the rewritten version are rescued from the original story's 19th and 21st paragraphs. That's too long to wait—those passages describe the disorder that is the story's focus and should appear early.

The revision's final sentence (*At least a dozen people in the United States have faced intense public scrutiny in the last decade after they said amnesia had . . . .*) was lifted verbatim from near the story's end. In the revision, that sentence provides the indispensable bridge from anecdotal introduction to story body. One could argue that this sentence could and should be the opening sentence. That's a matter for discussion and, perhaps, of personal preference. What we can say for sure is that one way to speed things up is to get to the point—if not immediately, then very soon.

As we see, slow anecdotal beginnings can get in the way of getting to the point. But nothing gets in the way of getting to the point like not *having* a point, or failing to express that point briefly and clearly, or interrupting the work on the way to the point. As I suggested repeatedly in the "guideline" section of this book, the simple, straightforward declarative sentence is the hero of good writing. Such a sentence has a main point to make and makes it. When sentences dither, distracted by tangential material, they become muddy and unreadable. Watch this magazine writer get lost on the way to his main point:

> The boutique art-house distributor Milestone Film & Video, which already deserves a medal for restoring and recirculating such lost classics as Mikhail Kalatozov's 'I am Cuba' and Pier Paolo Pasolini's 'Mamma Roma,' has released to video Powell's gorgeous 1937 first release, 'The Edge of the World' (beautifully restored by the British Film Institute), the story of two clans torn apart in a tiny Scottish Isles crofting community.

Read that sentence aloud. At 68 words, it's about three times as long as it should be. But its problem is not length so much as it is the hurdles you have to clear before you get to the period. Such writing is a snap to fix, though. All we have to do is remember what we learned in grade school—as well as what we read in the "guideline" section of this book: Clear sentences usually convey one main idea. That doesn't mean you can't include subordinate ideas when sentence length and content welcome them—we're not looking for Run-Dick-Run writing. But one *main* idea is usually all a sentence can bear, especially if the sentence also contains dense material such as titles and other proper nouns, arcane or "difficult" words, numbers, etc. Faster and more readable:

> *Powell's 1937 'Edge of the World,' beautifully restored by the British Film Institute, is available on video through arthouse distributor Milestone Film & Video. Milestone is the distributor that restored and recirculated such lost classics as Mikhail Kalatozov's 'I am Cuba' and Pier Paolo Pasolini's 'Mamma Roma.' Now it offers 'Edge of the World,' the story of two clans torn apart in a tiny Scottish Isles crofting community.*

The problem of obtrusive material is worsened in the original passage because it interrupts subject and verb *(distributor . . . has released)*. The demands of clarity suggest that subjects and verbs should be close together—as should verbs and objects. The frustrating habit of inserting all manner of material between naturally related parts of speech is endemic in fuzzy writing:

> *Working as part of an international team led by U.S. and Ethiopian scientists, a graduate student named Yohannes Haile-Selassie (no relation to the emperor), enrolled at the University of California, Berkeley, has found the remains of what appears to be the most ancient human ancestor ever discovered.*

In that passage, the writer interrupts subject and verb *(student . . . has found)* with the student's name, which unfortunately is a famous name and requires further explanation. Then he adds the annoyingly long university name as well. *Who* and *where* are important, but nothing is as important as writing well. The Ws—*who, what, when, where,* and *why*—can wait if they're going to get in the way of the message—as they do here. Again, the fix is easy:

> *A student at the University of California, Berkeley, has found the remains of what appears to be the most ancient human ancestor ever discovered. Ethiopian graduate student Yohannes Haile-Selassie—no relation to the emperor—made the discovery while working with an international team led by U.S. and Ethiopian scientists.*

Disturbing the flow between subject, verb, and object usually creates unwelcome speedbumps: "'It was an inducement for people to participate and a reward for their participation,' Ross, who will receive $75, said."

Reading that passage aloud shows what the eye missed: The solitary verb *said* hangs awkwardly at sentence end. Again, verbs like to snuggle up to their subjects. A small change restores order, even though the usual subject-verb structure becomes verb-subject: "'It was an inducement for people to participate and a reward for their participation,' said Ross, who will receive $75."

Here's a more typical disturbance in flow—and pace:

> *The accord between Bush and Rep. Charles Norwood of Georgia left Democrats—including the measure's co-sponsor, Rep. John Dingell, D-Dearborn—in the dark regarding what was agreed to.*
>
> *The problem leading to the marathon negotiations between Norwood, the White House and House Speaker Dennis Hastert, R-Ill., had been over provisions allowing patients to sue HMOs.*

The dashed insert in the first paragraph interrupts the natural flow of "left Democrats . . . in the dark." A similar speed-bump occurs in the second paragraph with the intervening material between subject and verb: "problem . . . had been." The ungrammatical "between" in the second paragraph ("between Norwood, the White House, and Hastert") also stops the reader. (*Between* refers to *two* entities.) Altogether, this brief passage offers a bumpy ride, but it can be smoothed easily when you recognize its structural problems:

> *The details of the accord between Bush and Rep. Charles Norwood eluded Democrats—including the measure's cosponsor, Rep. John Dingell, D-Dearborn.*
> *Whether patients could sue HMOs—and to what extent—was the issue that prolonged negotiations involving Norwood, the White House, and House Speaker Dennis Hastert, R-Ill.*

In short, a sentence is pulled off course when it meanders toward its destination, gathering stray bits along the way. But excessive length and faulty structure are just a couple of ways to slow the reader. At the other end of the spectrum is another definition of *slow*—the maddening practice of one-sentence-per-paragraph writing—often seen in journalistic writing, but elsewhere as well:

> *The ladies are on a mission.*
> *They board the bus and head to Oakville.*
> *The boxes are loaded, and the delivery is set.*
> *The bus arrives at the transitional care unit at the VA Health Care System.*

Periods and paragraphs should be among the reader's best friends, but in that passage they're speedbumps. One-sentence-per-paragraph writing is not only slow and space-eating, it's hardly writing at all. Writing means, in part, organizing information into families of related thought. In one-sentence-per-paragraph writing, every sentence is an orphan. Each has the same weight—it's unclear which is primary, which secondary; which is thesis, which support. The result is a barrage of unmoored statements in Run-Dick-Run syntax rather than a seamless flow of idea from paragraph to paragraph.

We often see radically shortened paragraphs in newspapers—chiefly because editors want to avoid long, gray blocks of type. That's a worthy goal, but it doesn't merit abandoning basic composition. Newspaper writers can paragraph more often than writers in other media and still shape the material. They can paragraph a single sentence for emphasis. But automatically hitting the return at every period is a sad substitute for purposeful and meaningful story organization.

Inexactitude in word choice also can hinder a reader's progress. When trying to create hitch-free writing, it helps to remember Mark Twain's admonition to use the right word, not its second cousin. A news story lauding a resident for bringing a large jazz festival to a tiny town says that generally only big cities are "hotbeds" of jazz. A *hotbed* is an environment that favors the rapid growth of something unsavory or undesirable: a hotbed of civil disobedience, a hotbed of drug use, of domestic violence, of petty crime. But a hotbed of *jazz*? Few would consider jazz a social ill.

A story about a Citizen of the Year award says the recipient was "duped" into attending the award ceremony. The reader stumbles over the word "duped," which means to deceive, gull, or fool for some nefarious purpose. Quicker, smoother, more exact phrasing for this context would be that the recipient was brought to the ceremony on a ruse, or that he was tricked into attending.

A novelist writes that a character "cavorted in her deck chair," and the reader stops long enough to wonder: Don't you at least have to get out of your chair to *cavort*?

Illogic as well as poor word choice slows the following passage, which is all speedbump: "Now, for the first time in many centuries, technology may have finally freed us of those wars that take over and dominate the national consciousness, while decimating entire generations."

The reader must clamber over "now, for the first time in many centuries, technology may have finally freed us." For the first time in many centuries? How much technology existed many centuries ago? Technology is a modern development—there wasn't another time, ever. Then the reader gets past the redundancy "take over and dominate" only to meet the trendy and often misused "decimate." *Decimate* means to destroy or eliminate a fraction of—namely, a tenth. Like many "dec" words, the meaning is built into the spelling—*decade, decimal, decapod* (10 legs), *decathlon* (10 events), *December* (the 10th month of the ancient Roman calendar). We can argue that *decimate* is so widely misused that its meaning may be changing, but controversial words or words in transition are not good choices because they stop many readers. The huge English lexicon offers many choices—words whose meanings are not in flux and that therefore mean the same thing to everyone. Those are the words careful writers seek. Why choose phrasing that has to be *defended*?

Here's a smoother, faster version of the fuzzy passage above: "Technology may have freed us from conventional war, which in the past consumed the whole country and annihilated an entire generation."

We've seen throughout this chapter that speedbumps often arise from intrusions and obtrusions. Unnecessary parenthetical or bracketed material is a major intrusion. So is a *"[sic]"* pointing out a mistake in a quotation (quotations containing mistakes can be paraphrased). So is the automatic insertion of title or age when either is beside the point: "He discussed the promotion with his wife, Mary Doe, 35, director of public relations at Acme Company, before he made his final decision." That comma-age-comma practice is useful in certain "just-the-facts" reports (if age matters), but it's a needless interruption in both form and content when striving for a conversational, story-telling style. How do we know? Because we don't talk that way. (In narrative or story-telling writing, at least, we should avoid all such "journalistic" obtrusions—such as "Mary Doe, D-Dallas." Conversational constructions are faster and smoother, even when longer: *Rep. Mary Doe, a Democrat from Dallas.*)

Granted, yesterday's readers were far more tolerant of both interruptions and a dense, discursive pace. But Dickensian sprawl and jitter apparently have little appeal for busy contemporary readers. Their response to authorly interruptions is likely to be *quiet please, we're trying to read!*

CHAPTER 22

Pace

Logic and Speedy Reading

That makes no sense and so do I.

—Daffy Duck

Let's capture the essence of *fast* in one broad statement: Speedy reading is *easy* reading. Easy *writing*, however, seldom equals easy reading. The chief engine of easy reading is conversational writing. Getting right to the point is also critical—no dithering!

So. All you have to do is "write as you speak"? No. That common admonition goes both too far and not far enough. Rather, we should write as we speak *when we speak well*: natural diction and syntax; plain, clear words; graceful, varied rhythms.

Following the guidelines in Section I helps yield speedy reading because those guidelines focus on making writing both clear and conversational. The handbook in Section III also helps because it focuses on making writing accurate. As we've seen, unclear, nonconversational, or inaccurate work is *always* slow. Beyond form, though, there's the all-important matter of *content*, and impeccable form must be married to impeccable content for the work to gain and keep momentum.

What are the earmarks of speedy content? Foremost are precision, logic, and sound reasoning—there's nothing *slower* than something that doesn't make sense. Also, appropriateness and interest. And, particularly in creative work, drama and excitement. In any case, the more stimulating the work, the faster it moves. It must be crafted, however, so that writer and reader move in lockstep—meaning that writers must keep the readers with them at all times. If the writer is slower than the reader, the reader gets impatient. If the writer gets ahead, readers may get lost.

Obviously, even well-crafted work will fail if the message is unacceptable or unacceptably presented. There's no benefit in crafting polished but idiotic statements. If the work is informational or expository, it must be clearly and logically presented and must anticipate and answer reader questions. If it's argumentation or criticism, it must be *sound* argument or criticism, or it will not persuade. If it's fiction—even science or fantasy fiction—it must be believable and consistent within its own world. Whatever the category, language and images should not go to war; metaphors shouldn't mix; analogies must be sensible and applicable.

Writers wanting to improve sometimes seek counsel: *I want to craft better narratives.* Or: *I'd like to be able to use metaphor and other literary devices more skillfully.* Or: *I'd like a more colorful style. A stronger voice. A more creative approach. Can you make some suggestions?*

Examining such work, one too often finds that those writers don't need to be better writers of narrative or metaphor or device. They just need to be better *writers*.

What do I mean by that rude suggestion?

Before embroidery comes the fabric. And the fabric of good writing is the tightly woven stuff of accuracy, clarity, brevity, precision, and logic. It may be human nature to want to be an artist before doing the tough and tedious work of learning the art's mechanics, but the effort is futile. It's like trying to play Beethoven before scales.

If good writing is the same thing as good speech, it also is the same thing as good thinking. Writing is so much a product of thinking that you cannot separate the two, and shoddy thought necessarily results in shoddy writing. According to George Orwell:

> *A man may take to drink because he feels himself to be a failure, and then fail all the more completely because he drinks. It is rather the same thing that is happening to the English language. It becomes ugly and inaccurate because our thoughts are foolish, but the slovenliness of our language makes it easier for us to have foolish thoughts.*

I recently read an editorial in a Texas newspaper defending the state's execution of a killer. The editorialist described the killer's hateful deeds and then asked triumphantly: "If we can't execute *him*, whom *can* we execute?" That question is poor argumentation because its underlying assumption is that we should be executing *somebody*, an assumption not shared by all. An argument that rests on false or unsupported assumption will fail to persuade all but those who hold the same *a priori* assumption—and it will offend or amuse those who do not.

Similarly, a fiction writer causes readers to balk by inappropriately bringing in the *deus ex machina*—literally, the god from the machine. The practitioner of *deus ex machina* is the fiction writer who gets stuck and solves his problem with an act of the gods rather than with a logical and believable solution. Pearl is tied to the railroad tracks, say, and the instant before the train cuts her to bits, a bolt of lightning strikes the engine, causing it to derail. Or the tracks of their own accord separate, causing the train to derail. Those are not credible solutions in the context of this story, which is grounded in reality and suddenly, inexplicably, goes supernatural. Now, if the story concerned Pearl's preternatural power over inanimate objects, that would be another matter. Again, action and behavior must be believable and consistent within its own world, and every story must act within its own rules if it is to gain the audience's "willing suspension of disbelief."

Here's a sports writer straining for voice and metaphor without giving much thought to accuracy or precision. "With respect comes pressure. Welcome to the real world. It's the double-edged sword in the hands of Canada's national women's hockey team."

That lead makes a claim: "With respect comes pressure." Let the writer prove *that*. But first, let him say it clearly: With *success* comes pressure. Saying it clearly should be easy because the lead's point is more obvious than profound. Yet the writer gets tangled in a not-very-tricky metaphor. His point is that the players' success has brought both more attention *and* more pressure. That success/pressure duo is the unnamed "it" of the third sentence—the double-edged sword.

So. Is that sword a weapon "in the hands of" the women's hockey team, as this writer asserts? Or is it hanging over their heads, à la the sword of Damocles? In creating an inaccurate and illogical metaphor, this writer misses an opportunity not only to use a logical one, but to pair it with a nice allusion as well.

Illogic, lack of logic, and loose connections do more than make readers scratch their heads—they drive readers away and damage the writer's credibility. Ponder the following beginning, for example:

> On Tuesday, Professor Juan Enrique Montez, exhorted his students to be honest, polite, and punctual. As always, he slammed his door shut the minute class began as a message to latecomers.
>
> On Wednesday, Juan Enrique Montez lay in a simple casket—the latest victim of Colombia's drug war.
>
> The story in La Prensa said simply, 'A Good Man Assassinated.'

What's the logical connection between the first paragraph and the second? Yes, on Tuesday, Montez was alive and on

Wednesday, he was dead—that's how it happens. But the readers expect something to come out of the first paragraph's references to Montez's words and actions—and nothing does.

Can logic be salvaged in this case? No. There's not even a tenuous link between the first two paragraphs, so it's best to scrap them. The third paragraph offers an interesting and functional beginning, and it would be a simple matter to link the newspaper headline's "good man" reference to Montez and to examples from his life of his "good man" behavior. (Although, I confess: the example we see in the lead is hardly persuasive. To teach politeness, he slams the door in his students' faces?)

Here's another wobbly socket: *Jim Norse, feeling every bit a 48-year-old man, began Wednesday with an aching back. He finished with another piece of history.*

Readers can only scratch their heads over such loose connections. Norse starts the day with a sore back and ends it with "another piece of history"? What's the *first* piece of history? Turns out Norse is an athlete who has set a couple of records. We don't know that, but even if we did, it wouldn't fix the illogic of the opening. The lead can be salvaged, however, if we tighten the connection: *At 48, Jim Norse could be history. Instead, he's making it.*

Whether in content or form, illogic has a way of sneaking past both writer and editor. A common problem is the non sequitur, a Latin term meaning "it does not follow." A non sequitur is an inference or conclusion that does not follow from the premise, or a comment unrelated to the preceding one.

In other words, a non sequitur is the essence of illogic.

Here's a common form of non sequitur: "Born in Boston, Smith began stealing from his clients before he had been in business a year." That's a non sequitur because Smith's birthplace has no bearing on his thievery, yet the sentence suggests a relationship.

Non sequiturs also can hide in *if/then* sentences. For example: "If you were at last year's film festival, then you know how

important the indie film is to the industry." The illogical inference: But if you *weren't* at last year's film festival, then you *don't*
know how important the indie is. Another:

> *Have you had a fresh, locally grown peach yet?*
> *If not, you'd better head for the orchard and have plenty of*
> *napkins handy.*
> *This year's peach crop is in its last couple of weeks with*
> *the big, red skins now ripe and the white ones about to ripen,*
> *said area peach growers.*

Again, the problem lies in the "if" contingency: If you
haven't had a peach, head for the orchard; if you *have* had one,
don't go? More logical: "If you love perfectly ripened peaches,
grab a handful of napkins and head for the orchard. This year's
red-skin peach crop is at its prime, says . . . ."

As those examples suggest, many problems in logic reside
in the flow of thought from one clause to another:

> *Since it's too early to make any solid declarations about*
> *where the Detroit Lions are headed—three games just isn't*
> *enough—there are some definite telltale signs.*
> *Unfortunately, those signals are conflicting.*

The *since* clause sets up the non sequitur in that lead. To
make the structure work, we'd have to write something like:
Since it's too early to make any solid declarations, we'll have to specu-
late. But that invites the reader to respond: If it's too early to make
declarations, why bother? Better: *It's too early to tell, but we can*
speculate. Or: *Although it's too early to tell, there are some signs . . . .*
But wait! If there are "definite" and "telltale" signals, it's *not* too
early to tell, is it? But wait again! If those "signals are conflicting," it *is* too early to tell.

What's the poor reader to think?

Avoid such hash by sticking with logical and coherent constructions: *It's hard to predict the Detroit Lions' direction this early in the season, but so far it looks like . . . .*

A single word can cause logic whiplash: "The two boys were hit in a spray of gunfire, police and witnesses said. No arrests have been made, but police say the suspects left the scene in two cars."

There were no arrests, *but* police say the suspects left the scene in two cars? Why are those two facts linked with *but*? One has no logical bearing on the other. (*With that construction, the reader expects something like: There were no arrests but police say they have several suspects.*) Better: "The two boys were hit in a spray of gunfire, and the suspects fled in two cars, said police, who have made no arrests in the case."

Snarled logic sometimes has less to do with the flow of thought from clause to clause than with the flow of thought, period. Consider this sentence from a newspaper profile: "He has the relaxed self-confidence of a Port Arthur Eagle Scout who's tried hard all his life and been good."

Where's the logic in such a statement? What would it mean to have the relaxed self-confidence of a *Port Arthur Eagle Scout?* Is that a *category*? More logical: "He has the relaxed self-confidence of one who has, for his lifelong, tried hard and been good."

Illogical word pairs also cause trouble: "Traffic jams, a pesky scourge in Dallas and other big cities across the nation, often survive attempts to eradicate them."

Pesky means annoying or irksome; *scourge* means a calamity or affliction. Should we pair those words? Would we speak of a "bothersome catastrophe" or an "annoying cataclysm"? Recast for linguistic logic: "That big-city bane, the traffic jam, often outlasts the construction meant to correct it."

Another problem in logic arises with mishandled figurative expressions:

> *You can't blame the network for the rain, except that this is standard fare now, tipping these big-time golf events back closer and closer to prime time. They are cutting it too close to the vest . . .*

Idiom alert! The expression is *"playing* it close to the vest," which means holding one's cards where they cannot be seen—thus, being sly or secretive. That sense has no meaning in this context, but "cutting it too close to the vest" has no meaning in *any* context. The writer probably means "cutting it too close to the *bone."*

The following passage shows the lack of careful thought almost always attendant in illogic:

> *Louis Armstrong is, arguably, the most influential artist in popular music. Ever. Without the audacious records he made 75 years ago, the music we enjoy today—be it jazz or rap or techno-death metal—would be a lot more stiff and sedate, if it existed at all.*

Before we discuss the illogic of that passage, let's consider the fashionable weasel word *arguably.* It means . . . *what? Maybe yes, maybe no. Could be. Might be. We could argue that. I can't prove it, but.* The word, unwelcome in any authoritative work, makes this passage an odd amalgam of the tentative and assertive.

And the assertion is as sweeping and illogical as it is insupportable. Let's strip bare the claim: *Without the music Satchmo made 75 years ago, the music we enjoy today would be a lot more stiff and sedate, if it existed at all.*

Now consider:

- If Charlemagne hadn't existed, no one would have dreamed up the stirrup.
- Without Gutenberg, we wouldn't have printed media.
- Without Picasso's creations, all our art, whether canvas or sculpture, would still be representative.

We cannot say—*no one* can say—what would have happened if what happened hadn't happened. Such statements are not only beyond the ability of surmise, they're also irresponsible and profitless. Can we guess? Sure. But why bother? Dealing with what *did* happen is infinitely more productive than whimsy.

In sum, there are as many kinds of *slow* as there are ways to impede the readers' progress. But illogic is the worst kind—it not only halts readers, it backs them up and chases them away.

A HANDBOOK

CHAPTER 23

A Language Handbook

A Brief (But Not Necessarily Easy) Quiz

A person who misuses the language is as bereft of good taste as someone who picks his nose at a party.

—John Simon

Below are some sentences with common grammar and punctuation problems that trouble many people. Can you find the problems? This is a straightforward quiz, not meant to be tricky or even especially tough; it merely comprises frequent complaints. Explanations follow *(don't peek!),* as does a primer on those pesky pronouns, the part of speech responsible for most grammar gaffes in both speech and writing.

1. If I was rich, I'd do something about the homeless.
2. The administration hopes the faculty will set their own goals.
3. We feel badly that we missed your call.
4. You've been here longer than me.
5. You'll prefer our plan because of it's homeowner protections.
6. Leave the parcel with whomever is in reception.
7. He lived in an old, red brick house.

8. They snuck over the wall.
9. Her husband John loves sushi.
10. The door prize will go to the Smith's because they arrived early.
11. The director gave bonuses to Sally and myself.
12. I appreciate you doing this for me.
13. This gift will show someone you care about them.
14. I want to lay on the beach awhile.
15. Twain wrote, "Nothing so needs reforming as other people's habits".
16. We stayed outdoors like we did when we were young.
17. He is one of those people who always wants the last word.
18. As far as the budget, I see no problem.
19. The emphasis is on content, but form is equally as important.
20. In high school, Jansen was named as the most likely to succeed.

Answers

1. **If I *were* rich.** The subjunctive *were*, not *was*, is needed in "if" clauses that are contrary to fact—or when expressing desire or supposition: I wish I *were* going. If it *were* up to them, nobody would go.

2. **The administration hopes the faculty will set *its* own goals.** Or: hopes the faculty *members* will set *their* . . . . The error here is a pronoun/antecedent agreement problem. The antecedent *faculty* is a collective, singular noun—an "it," not a "they." *Their* does not agree with *faculty*, and therefore we must change either the antecedent or the pronoun. (More on pronouns later in the "pronoun primer.")

3. **Feel *bad*.** Use adjectives rather than adverbs with sense verbs or with linking verbs such as forms of the verb *to be, seem, appear, become,* etc.: *This food smells bad. It looks bad.* The adverb *badly* describes action (adverbs modify verbs): "He swam *badly* in the second race." But the adjective *bad* describes

condition or passive states: "He felt *bad* when he lost the race." (*Bad* modifies *he,* the subject, rather than the verb *swam.*) She feels *stupid,* not "stupidly"; looks *pretty,* not "prettily"; seems *nice,* not "nicely."

4. **Longer than I.** This sentence means: "You've been here longer than I (have)," so we want the subjective *I,* not the objective *me.* We would not say, "You've been here longer than *me has.*" (More on pronouns later in the "pronoun primer.")

5. *Its.* Like other possessives—*his, hers, ours, theirs, etc.*—*its* has no apostrophe. *It's* (with an apostrophe) is a contraction of "it is." (*It's* can also mean "it has," as in "It's been a long time.")

6. **With *whoever* is in reception.** When *whoever* or *whomever* seems to be both object and subject (here, the object of *with* and the subject for *is),* choose *whoever. Whoever* is the subject for *is,* and the whole *whoever* clause is the object of *with.* (More on pronouns in the "pronoun primer.")

7. **An old red brick house**—No comma. The mistake of automatically placing commas between adjectives preceding nouns is widespread among even professional writers. Here, *old* modifies "red brick house"; *old* and *red brick* are not separate and equal modifiers. When in doubt, place *and* between the adjectives. If the result seems odd, you don't want a comma. "Old *and* red brick house"—no, it's odd, so no comma. "A beautiful *and* baby girl"—again, it's odd, so no comma: *beautiful baby girl.* However, "a large *and* ugly dog" sounds fine, so we would write *large, ugly dog.*

8. *Sneaked.* "Snuck" is as despised as it is common, and you wonder how it even came to be—it doesn't follow usual forms. The floor *creaked,* not "cruck"; the roof *leaked,* not "luck"; the storm *peaked,* not "puck." *Sneak* behaves the way those verbs behave, so *sneaked* is the preferred past tense.

9. **Her husband, John, loves sushi.** We use commas to set off words identifying a preceding noun or pronoun when those words add parenthetical, nonessential information. We'd omit the commas around *John* only if she had more than one husband at the same time—her husband John as opposed to her husband

Harry. (Yes, it's illegal, but it happens.) If she had more than one husband, then *which* husband we're referring to would become essential information, and we'd skip the commas. *Note:* If she is divorced or a widow, she may have had multiple husbands. The practice in such cases is to refer to a "former" or "ex" husband, or to a "late" husband—and we'd still use the commas if she had just one former or deceased husband. If she had more than one of either, the commas would be omitted: Her late husband John; her former husband John.

10. *Smiths.* The word is plural, not possessive. If my mail is any indication, the "wild" apostrophe makes people breathe fire.

11. **To Sally and *me*.** Stripping *Sally* from this sentence shows the problem: *gave bonuses to myself.* We need the object *me*. The word *myself* is neither subject nor object. "Myself gave a bonus to him" is as flawed as "he gave a bonus to myself." (More on pronouns in the "pronoun primer" below.)

12. **I appreciate *your* doing this.** Use possessive pronouns before gerunds. (Gerunds are words that end in "ing" but act as nouns. "Doing" is a gerund in this sentence.)

13. **Show someone you care about *him* (or *her*).** This, like No. 2, is a pronoun/antecedent problem. Words ending in "one" and "body" (*someone, everyone, anyone, somebody, everybody, anybody,* etc.) are singular and should be followed by singular pronouns rather than by the plural *they, their,* or *them*. Many don't want to use the masculine pronoun as a generic term applying to both sexes, however, and "he or she" is bulky and awkward. It's not necessary to do either; there's always a better way. Here, we could say simply, "Show someone you care." (More on pronouns in the "pronoun primer.")

14. *Lie* **on the beach.** The verb "to lie" means to rest or recline, while the verb "to lay" means to place or put. A complication is that *lay* also is the past tense of *lie,* but this sentence is not in past tense.

15. **". . . habits."** In American English, periods and commas go *inside* quotation marks. (In Great Britain, however, the practice is to put periods and commas outside quotation marks.)

16. **Stayed outdoors *as* we did when we were young.** *Like* would be correct if this sentence were rendered: "We stayed outdoors like kids." The *like* and *as* matter is simple if we remember that *like* is not a conjunction. Use it as a preposition to compare nouns and pronouns (she looks like *him*; it looks like a *disaster*). Use *as* (or *as if* or *as though*) to introduce clauses (a group of words containing both subject and verb). For example: He shrieked *like* a maniac. He shrieked *as if* he'd lost his mind.

17. **He is one of those people who always *want* the last word.** This common error comes from the assumption that *one* is the subject for the verb *want* (one wants). In fact, the subject for *want* is *who*, which in turn refers to *people*—therefore: people *want*. This sort of sentence is saying: "Of all those people who always want to have the last word, he is one."

18. **As far as the budget *is concerned*.** "As far as" is incomplete without the words necessary to complete the thought: as far as something *is concerned*, or as far as something *goes*. Another way to deal with unfinished "as far as" structures is to change them to "as for": *As for the budget . . . .*

19. **But form is equally important** [no *as*]. The ungrammatical "equally *as*" is yet another problem with the tiny word *as*. For example, a restaurant critic wrote that he liked the beef, but the veal was "equally *as* good." The veal was equally good, and that's what he should have written.

20. **Jansen was named the most likely to succeed** [no *as*]. *As* often incorrectly follows such verbs as *named, called, elected,* etc.: "The association elected her *as* president." That's like saying: "The parents named their new baby *as* John." Omit *as*: "The association elected her president"; "Jansen was named most likely to succeed."

A pronoun primer

Getting clear on pronouns would solve most of our common grammar problems. Few gaffes generate as much heat as confusing the subjective pronouns *I, he, she, we,* or *they* with the objective pronouns *me, him, her, us,* or *them.*

- A university professor says regarding the cost of the election per voter: "It bothers people inside the beltway and attentive watchers *like you and I* more than it does regular folks."
- Another professor—oblivious of the irony in his own comment—says that the only people in his department who care about grammar "are two other instructors and *myself.*"
- A newspaper columnist: "I notice that *you and her* have the same last name."
- A TV home decorating show: "The new office makes a wonderful workplace *for Sherry and I.*"
- An editor: "This is *between you and I.*"
- A professional writer: "They introduced the new director *to him and I.*"
- An entertainment reporter: "She's at least 15 years older than *him.*"
- A radio commentator: "My wife has a better memory than *me.*"
- A headline: "*Who* do you trust?"
- A newscaster: "Baker acknowledged that it was *him* who sent the anonymous note."

Each of those examples is ungrammatical. It seems we all remember that it's wrong to say, "Johnny and me are going"—just as wrong as "me is going." It's wrong because we need a subject, and *me* is an object. We naturally say, "*I* am going," but "Call *me.*" We're so suspicious of "Johnny and me," however, that we may avoid it even when it's right. For example, we might say: *Call Johnny and I. Give it to Johnny and I. Tell Johnny and I.* If we take *Johnny* out of those sentences, though, we see how wrong *I* is—as wrong as *call I, give it to I, tell I.*

The pronoun errors in the examples above are just variations on the same theme. The pronoun we choose depends upon whether it should be subjective or objective. If it's the actor (a subject), it should be *I, he, she, they, we, who.* If it's acted upon (an object), it should be *me, him, her, them, us, whom.*

"Self" pronouns are different from other pronouns because they are neither subjects nor objects, but reflexives (*I* hurt *myself*) or intensifiers (*they* are going, but *I myself* am staying home). Again, if we would not say, "Myself is going," we likewise must not say, "John and myself are going." If we would not say, "Let myself know," we likewise must not say, "Let John or myself know."

Removing other people from the sentence and letting the pronoun stand alone quickly reveals which role the pronoun is playing—subject or object. Substituting other pronouns also can help in certain sentences. For example, if we know that it is right to say, "This is between *us,*" then we also know it is right to say, "This is between you and *me*"—because *us* is objective, and any pronoun we choose for this particular sentence would also have to be objective. "This is between you and *I*" is the same thing as "This is between *we.*"

Pronouns in "than" sentences are easy. If you can place a verb after the pronoun, and it makes sense, choose the subjective pronoun: *He's older than I [am]; I've worked here longer than she [has].* We would not say *older than me [am], worked here longer than her [has].*

The newscaster's "Baker acknowledged that it was *him* who sent the anonymous note," shows the common problem of using an objective pronoun after some form of "to be"—*is, are, was, were, been.* The preferred practice is to follow a "be" verb with a *subjective* pronoun: *This is she. Was it he? It is he who should apologize.* If that seems over-fastidious, we can always use a proper noun rather than a pronoun: *This is Mary. Was it John? It is Frank who should apologize.*

Some experts say it's high time we accepted such structures as *it is me, that's her, it's him.* I don't disagree, especially in speech, but the problem is our audience. Many see those constructions as wrong and—worse—ignorant. That perception is hazardous to any communicator but especially in writing, even in such "informal" workplace communication as email, which is often printed, distributed to others, and—sadly—lasts forever. A mistake in writing is a mistake in a possibly permanent record—in which the real or perceived error remains to offend again and again. The writer's *message* is damaged when the reader gets caught up in form rather than content.

The best solution to such problems is to use neither a construction that might be seen as ungrammatical nor one that might be seen as stiff or stuffy. We can always write around the problem. In the "Baker" sentence above, for example, the writer could have deleted "it was he" and said simply: "Baker acknowledged that he sent the anonymous note." Both in speech and in writing, such choices are easy, quick, *and* correct.

Who/Whom

The headline *"Whom do you trust?"* means the same thing as "You trust *whom?"* We need that objective *whom* because we would correctly say: You trust *me, him, her, them, us.* "Who do you trust" is the same as saying: You trust *I, he, she, they, we.*

Again, we can cut through *who* and *whom* confusion if we remember that the pronoun's form depends upon whether the word acts as a subject or an object. *Who* and *whoever* are subjective; *whom* and *whomever* are objective. We can usually decide what's right by restructuring the sentence to make a statement—rather than a question—or by substituting other subjective or objective pronouns for *who* and *whom.* (Subjective: *I, he, she, they, we.* Objective: *me, him, her, them, us.*) For example:

- Who/whom is going? We would say *he* or *she* is going, so we need the subjective *who*. Correct: *Who is going?*
- Who/whom did you say is going? Restructured, this sentence says: "You did say *he/she* is going?" So again we need the subjective *who*. We might miss this because we forget that we need a subject (*who*) for the verb *is going.* Correct: *Who did you say is going?*

210

- There's the man who/whom police are investigating. The police are investigating *him (objective),* so we likewise need the objective *whom.* Correct: *There's the man whom police are investigating.*
- We wondered who/whom they would elect. They would elect *him, her, them;* we need the objective *whom.* Correct: *We wondered whom they would elect.*

While the errors above are straightforward grammar and punctuation errors, some mistakes arise because of myths and misperceptions regarding the proper use of the language. We'll discuss those linguistic "hobgoblins" next.

CHAPTER 24

A Language Handbook

Dispelling the Myths

In writing, it's not wise to violate rules until you know how to observe them.

—T.S. Eliot

We could expand upon T. S. Eliot's remark: Yes, but knowing how to observe the rules means first knowing what the rules *are*. My years as a writing teacher and professional writing coach have taught me that there's far too much traffic in linguistic myth even among educators and professional wordsmiths. Baseless hobgoblins, misperceptions, and taboos are often passed on by folks who have accepted them as fact. Sometimes a simple suggestion from a teacher or editor becomes a *rule*. Sometimes a rule is fairly stated, but its application is misunderstand. Whatever the cause, we too often hold mistaken notions about the proper use of the language.

By linguistic myth, I mean stating as a rule of language something that is not only *not* a rule but in fact has no support (and may never have had) among grammarians or other language experts. What are some common myths? All of the following, which say we *should not*:

- split infinitives or verb phrases
- end sentences with prepositions

- start sentences with *and* or *but*
- use contractions in "formal" communication
- use a comma before *and* in a list (the serial or Oxford comma)
- treat *none* and *couple* as plurals

That same kind of mythology says we should avoid the word *that* whenever possible, and *that* (See? We need it.) we should use the article "an" before *historian, historic,* or *historical*. None of that is true, and none of it is supported by language experts. At this moment, you may be lathering yourself into a high dudgeon: *What does she mean by this heresy? Why, I was taught that . . . .* So let me say it again: *None of that is true, and none of it is supported by language experts.* It's high time we stopped scaring people with these bugbears.

Let's consider them one at a time.

Split infinitives

The infinitive is *to* plus a verb: *to walk, to go, to arrive, to leave,* etc. A split infinitive: *to slowly walk, to boldly go, to eventually arrive, to hurriedly leave.* Split infinitives are often unattractive, which is reason enough not to split them unnecessarily, but they are not *wrong.* How did such a widespread notion get started? In the 1800s, wordsmiths tried to make English conform to Latin, and in Latin the infinitive is one word and *cannot* be split. But we occasionally *must* split the infinitive in English, and it's absurd to say you *cannot* do what you *must* do.

We are right to split an infinitive when the unsplit version is clumsy or unclear. For example: "The dean is considering adding a course *to better prepare* students for the test." Should we write "a course better to prepare"? Or "a course to prepare better students"? We could place *better* after *students* (to prepare students better for the test), but the most precise placement splits the infinitive: *to better prepare students.*

Watch what occurs when you try to unsplit the following split infinitives:

"The CEO expects profits to more than double next year." Expects profits *more than to double*? Expects profits *to double more than*?

"The group plans to legally ban open disclosures." Plans legally *to ban open disclosures*? Plans *to ban legally open* disclosures?

"We hope to strongly protest passing the legislation." We hope *strongly to protest* passing? Hope *to protest strongly passing*?

In short, we should lay the split infinitive superstition to rest. Avoid splitting it when it gets in the way of grace and precision and split away when it *preserves* grace and precision.

Split verb phrases

Another unsupportable notion is that there's something wrong with split compound verbs (*should* probably *go*, *will* never *be*). Like the split infinitive, the split verb phrase is not wrong, but unlike the split infinitive, the split verb phrase is seldom unattractive. Good communicators split them all the time. Again, we should avoid *awkward* splits: "He's repairing the computer that she *had* several weeks ago *given* to the church" should be "repairing the computer that she *had given* to the church several weeks ago." But "the plan *was summarily dismissed*" is fine—better, in fact, than "the plan summarily was dismissed," or "the plan was dismissed summarily."

Here are sentences from professional writers that show the sort of odd word order that often results from trying not to split verb phrases: "Sally knew that Harriet *privately had contributed* substantial sums to the high school for students' lunches and fees." Splitting the verb, as we doubtless would in speech, yields more natural phrasing: "Sally knew that Harriet *had privately contributed* substantial sums to the high school . . . ." Another example: "She could see that Sheila *even had polished* the salt cellars." More natural: "She could see that Sheila *had even polished* the salt cellars." Or one might preserve both verb phrase and logic with: "She could see that Sheila *had polished even* the salt cellars."

Ending a sentence with a preposition

Winston Churchill—a clear, readable, and articulate writer and speaker—was once scolded for ending sentences with prepositions. He supposedly responded: *Madam, this is arrant pedantry up with which I will not put.*

That story may be apocryphal, but it makes a solid point. No rule says you can't end a sentence with a preposition. Again, if the practice is clumsy and artificial, that's reason enough not to do it. But if it's not clumsy and artificial, why make it so by conforming to some imaginary rule?

Here's where that imaginary rule takes us. We could no longer say: *You don't know what you're talking about.* We would say, instead: *You don't know about what you're talking.* We couldn't ask: *Is that the tradition in the town you come from?* We would ask, instead: *Is that the tradition in the town from which you come?* We couldn't say: *It was perfectly clear what they were up to.* We would say, instead: *It was perfectly clear to what they were up.* No, that still ends with a preposition. Then, we must say instead: *It was perfectly clear up to what they were.*

Sometimes those protesting prepositions at the ends of sentences cite as an example: "Where is it at?" But the fault with that sentence is not that it ends with a preposition; it's that it's a gross redundancy. The sentence should be "Where is it?" Period.

Starting sentences with *and* or *but*

Writers sometimes run into a prejudice against beginning sentences with such connective words as *and, but, for, however, nevertheless, now, still,* and *yet.* But that's all it is, a prejudice—and an unfounded one. Beginning sentences with such words is not wrong and, to the contrary, is often attractive—it not only offers continuity and transition, but it also allows the writer to end the previous sentence, which may be growing overlong. Finally, sentences beginning with *and* or *but* are more emphatic because of the conjunction: "I am going to hear my boss' speech. *But* that doesn't mean I *want* to."

The practice of beginning sentences with connective words is nothing new. The Oxford English Dictionary offers examples from schooled writers as far back as the 10th century, and the Bible contains many such sentences.

One caution: Be careful not to overuse the device. It should not seem an affectation.

Contractions

Failing to use contractions even when they would best serve the sentence is a writing flaw fueled by a common myth. Some writers have been taught to use whole words in professional or "formal" communications—*do not, cannot, I will, we have, it is,* etc.—instead of *don't, can't, I'll, we've, it's.*

That idea probably originated in the spurious notion that "formal" writing, with its stiff, nonconversational style, somehow is more suited to professional communication than "informal" writing. Some computer grammar checkers can shoulder the blame, too. But grammar checkers are notorious for mistakes and silly suggestions. (Artificial intelligence is no doubt wonderful, but sometimes we need the real thing.)

Fact is, both contractions and whole words are perfectly fine. Whether we choose one over the other depends upon the sentence—its rhythms, phrasing, length, emphasis, and pace. We should prefer whatever sounds better, whatever is seamless, natural, fast. In short, there's nothing particularly "colloquial" about contractions—good writers use them in every kind of writing.

How absurd is avoiding contractions? In the last sentence of the preceding paragraph, should I have written: "In short, *there is* nothing particularly 'colloquial' about contractions"? Why? Reading the sentence aloud shows that it moves faster and smoother with the contraction *there's.* A box on the front of *The Wall Street Journal* bears this headline: "What's News." Should that be changed to "What Is News"? Obviously not. If I'm writing to Aunt Jane, I might say: "We're leaving Tuesday, but don't worry, we'll see you before we go." If that sentence appeared in a "formal" communication, should it be *"We are* leaving Tuesday, but *do not* worry, *we will* see you before we go"?

The sentences below are from excellent writers who understand the use and benefits of contractions. Read both versions aloud and see how contractions can smooth sentence flow and preserve speed, focus, and grace:

"Let's not rush to judgment before we're sure there's a problem." This sentence would be slow and cumbersome if it were rendered: *"Let us* not rush to judgment before *we are* sure *there is* a problem."

"It's to the place now where it's more fun to stay home, but don't admit it." Awkward: *"It is* to the place now where *it is* more fun to stay home, but *do not* admit it."

Below, on the other hand, are passages from writers who apparently fear contractions. Again, read the two versions aloud, and hear the improvement in the second version:

"Although *it is* hard to predict how this controversy will end, *there is* clearly a shift in opinion." A version using contractions would be better: "Although it's hard to predict how this controversy will end, there's clearly a shift in opinion."

"There is nothing wrong with getting rich as long as *it is* done fairly." Better: "There's nothing wrong with getting rich as long as it's done fairly."

If contractions are so great, should we use them to the exclusion of whole words? Absolutely not. We need both. Whole words sometimes are better in certain cases because they are more emphatic or stately: *I cannot tolerate that. This will not stand.* And it's probably best to avoid ambiguous contractions such as *he'd, we'd, I'd,* etc., because they mean not only *he would, we would, I would,* but also *he had, we had, I had.* (However, *it's* is acceptable for both *it is* and *it has:* "It's good to see you; it's been a long time.").

Otherwise, contract away. Your style will be smoother, faster, and friendlier for it.

Restoring the serial comma

A common myth is that there's something wrong with the serial or "Oxford" comma—that is, the comma before *and* or *or* in a list. That myth is especially prevalent among media writers, most of whom use the Associated Press Stylebook. That stylebook may have unwittingly contributed to the confusion by saying it's OK to omit the serial comma in a simple list: *The flag is red, white and blue. He would nominate Tom, Dick or Harry.* But AP style also demands the serial comma when the series is complex, or when the last two items run together ambiguously, or when an item in the list contains a conjunction. Examples:

> *The main points to consider are whether the athletes are skillful enough to compete, whether they have the stamina to endure the training, and whether they have the proper attitude.*
> *I had orange juice, toast, and ham and eggs for breakfast.*

The gist of the AP guideline is that we should retain the serial comma in all but the simplest and shortest list, and it does not say that the serial comma is wrong in any case. But that's not the way the guideline has been assimilated. Instead, some writers have concluded—entirely without support—that the serial comma is wrong and should be deleted. But it's not wrong, and no accepted authority would say that it is.

Interestingly, even those who would in some cases delete the serial comma require in all cases the serial *semi-colon*—an even heavier separator than the comma. That doesn't make sense, and such inconsistencies point to a style practice that causes more trouble than it's worth. And it isn't worth anything. Omitting the serial comma destroys parallel balance, forces writers to decide whether this is one of those times when the serial comma is optional, and often muddies meaning.

Writing authorities agree that the serial comma should be retained in all cases. Here are excerpts from experts:

In their revered *Elements of Style,* William Strunk and E.B. White write that in a series of three or more terms with a single conjunction, commas should separate the terms, including before the conjunction. Examples: *Red, white, and blue. Gold, silver, or copper. He opened the letter, read it, and made a note of its contents.*

Modern American Usage, Wilson Follet, *et. al.*: This entry is five pages long, with many examples showing the resulting confusion of omitting serial commas. An excerpt:

"A widely parroted dictum is supposed to settle the issue: If you have the conjunction, you don't need the comma. That is bad reasoning or no reasoning at all. A conjunction is a connective device, as its name announces; whereas a mark of punctuation is nothing if not separative. To insist that the first perform the duty of the second is like prescribing sand in the bearings . . . . It is implicit in the standard form of a series that when you write *red, white, and blue*, you mean *red and white and blue*—three equal terms . . . . The recommendation here is to use the comma between *all* members of a series, including the last two, on the common-sense ground that to do so will preclude ambiguities and annoyances."

From Modern English Usage, H.W. Fowler: "Where more than two words or phrases or groupings occur together in a sequence, a comma should precede the *and* . . . . The 'Oxford' comma is frequently, but in my view, unwisely, omitted by many."

From The Chicago Manual of Style: "When a conjunction joins the last two elements in a series, a comma is used before the conjunction. Examples: *Attending the conference were Farmer, Johnson, and Kendrick. We have a choice of copper, silver, or gold. The owner, the agent, and the tenant were having an acrimonious discussion.*

The Chicago Manual adds that in a "series of short independent clauses, the last two of which are joined by a conjunction, a comma should be placed between the clauses and before the conjunction. Example: *Harris presented the proposal to the gover-*

nor, the governor discussed it with the senator, and the senator made an appointment with the president."

The following also agree that the serial comma should be retained:

- The Columbia Guide to Standard American English
- Webster's Ninth New Collegiate Dictionary
- Webster's New World Dictionary (The Associated Press' dictionary of choice)
- The U.S. Government Printing Office's Manual of Style
- The Modern Language Association's *Line by Line,* by Claire Cook.
- The McGraw-Hill Style Manual
- The Copy Editor's Handbook, by Amy Einsohn
- Shipley's Style Guide for the Workplace

These sources document the unchanging preference for using serial commas. Nor has anything changed. The recently published Dictionary of Modern American Usage, by Bryan Garner, says that a comma "separates items (including the last from the next-to-last) in a list of more than two—e.g.: 'The Joneses, the Smiths, and the Nelsons.' Whether to include the serial comma has sparked many arguments. But it's easily answered in favor of inclusion because omitting the final comma may cause ambiguities, whereas including it never will."

Why do some journalists hang onto a practice that the rest of the literate world either never heard of or rejects? Habit and tradition. Nothing else, and nothing better. (A newsroom copy editor actually told me it was to save space. Please. Prune one redundancy, delete one unnecessary word—we'd make enough room for a handful of serial commas.) For clarity, balance, and beauty, restore the serial comma to your work. There was never good reason to omit it.

None and *couple*

Another common myth is that the words *none* and *couple* are always singular.

We're sometimes taught that *none* means "no one" or "not one." But it also means "not any" (the pronoun *any* is both singular and plural), and it also can refer to *some* or *several*. If this were not so, "none of the members *is* going" would be a correct construction, and it obviously is not. We should use *none* as singular or plural depending upon the construction. If the word clearly means *no one* or *not one*, it's singular: *Of the five candidates, none is qualified.* The stress here is on *not one* of the candidates. If the stress is on *not any*, it's plural: *None of the department heads, managers, or executives are receiving bonuses.* When the stress is on more than one, it's plural: *None were more pleased with his arrest than his former friends.* The stress here is on *all* his former friends. Also, if the noun following *none* is plural and cannot be construed as singular, treat *none* as plural: *None of the queen's dresses were suitable.* But: *None of the queen's clothing was suitable.*

Couple also is singular or plural depending upon the sentence. If each person in the couple is acting individually, even though in concert with the other, the word is plural: *The couple are seeing their divorce lawyers.* (Consider the sentence that would result if *couple* were always singular: "The couple is seeing its divorce lawyers.") *Couple* is singular, however, if the two people are acting as one: "The couple *is* giving millions to the university."

In American English, collective nouns are generally singular, however—*company, team, jury, committee, faculty*, and so forth. That means each is an *it*, not a *they*. That creates problems when a collective noun is made up of people: the word *it* can be awkward. It's best in such cases to add a plural noun to the collective noun—instead of *faculty*, make it faculty *members*; instead of *company*, make it company *employees* or *managers,* or whoever. Then the pronoun that follows will not be *it*, but *they*—a word we can gracefully apply to living beings.

The British have no problem with collective nouns. They simply make them plural: *The jury are deliberating, the committee are planning, the faculty were present.* That tradition makes a lot of linguistic sense, but it's not the tradition of American English.

Keeping *that*

The word *that* has a bad reputation among some writers and editors, but it doesn't deserve it. Obviously, any unnecessary word is unnecessary. But we can damage clarity and precision by carelessly deleting a needed *that*. For example:

> *He said technicians later discovered the fire near the control center burned out a section of the cable that relays information between trains and the center.*

Some sentences need a *that* for flow and sense, and this is one. It seems to say on first reading that the technicians discovered the *fire*, when what they actually discovered was that the fire burned out a section of the cable. This confusion can be avoided by placing *that* after *discovered*:

> *He said technicians later discovered that the fire near the control center burned out a section of the cable that relays information between trains and the center.*

Retain *that* with sentences that contain both attribution and time: *Our CEO said Wednesday he would step down.* Did the CEO say it Wednesday, or will he step down Wednesday? A *that* would clarify the meaning: "Our CEO said Wednesday *that* he would step down," or "Our CEO said *that* Wednesday he would step down."

Also consider retaining *that* following such words as *announce, believe, thought, reveal, declare, understand, assert, assume, allege,* and the like. "He announced a report accusing her of lying was false" is confusing on first reading and is clearer as: "announced *that* a report accusing her of lying was false." The same is true of "They believe the chief witness in this case will take the stand this week." That sentence is clearer as: "They believe *that* the chief witness in this case will take the stand this week."

A and *an*

You wouldn't think such little words as "a" and "an" could cause much confusion, but they do. We don't use "a" before a vowel sound or "an" before a consonant sound—"a eagle," "a incident," "an gratuity," or "an historic," for example.

Seems a small thing, but it makes people grit their teeth. It's a wonder that such mistakes with "a" and "an" happen at all, because the faulty form is harder to say that the correct form: *an eagle, an incident, a gratuity, a historic.* That's because vowel sounds glide effortlessly into consonant sounds, and vice versa, but they fight when butted against their own kind. Say aloud "an airplane" and "a airplane," and "a book," and "an book," and you'll hear what I mean.

Still, we hear "an historic" or "an historical" all the time. A politician refers to a conference as "an historic" meeting, and a news anchor describes someone as "an historic" figure.

"An historic" is faulty because we sound the *H,* a consonant. Only when the *H* is silent do we use "an": *an heir, an honor* (but *a hair).*

The problem with *H* is more common when the stress falls on the second syllable—thus such questionable phrasing as *an habitual criminal, an hypothesis,* or *an heroic.* Although the *H* may be weak in such structures, it is *not* silent, and that settles the argument. As Bryan Garner writes in *Modern American Usage, an* before such words is "likely to strike readers and listeners as affectations." (The practice is probably more accepted in Great Britain, although even there R.W. Fowler, a leading authority on English usage, wrote nearly 80 years ago that "opinion is divided" regarding *H* words with unstressed first syllables.)

A similar error is seen with the word *humble,* in which the *H* is also sounded. But the problem here is that some fail to sound the *H,* pronouncing it "umble." Thus, they say "an *umble* person"—observing the rule of using "an" before a vowel sound, but incorrectly using the vowel sound. I know of no dictionary whose preferred pronunciation for *humble* or *humbly* is "umble" or "umbly."

Sometimes people protest such phrasing as: "A*n FBI* investigation started the whole mess." Or "It's *an NCAA* policy." Or "She has *an MA* degree." They object that the article "an" is wrong because it precedes the consonants F, N, and M. But that's a misstatement of the rule. As we saw above, we use "a" before a consonant *sound* and "an" before a vowel *sound.* It's true that F, N, and M are consonants, and we would use "a" before the words *federal, national,* and *master's.* But here they are part of abbreviations, and they *sound* like "eff," "enn," and "emm."

By the same token, words beginning with vowels that sound like consonants take "a." Thus, it's *a eulogy* (the EUL sounds like *yule*), *a uniform* (the U sounds like *you*), or *a Ouija board* (the OUI sounds like *we*). It's *an herb* or *an herbal* (the *h-* is preferably silent in American English, although not in British English), but *a herbicide* (the *h-* is sounded).

American English made no clear distinction between "a" and "an" before the 1800s. The U.S. Constitution refers to "an uniform" rule of naturalization, for example. But for the last century at least, we've let the whole matter of "a" or "an" rest on pleasing the ear and tongue—it's as difficult to say "a hour" or "an history book" as it is unattractive to hear.

Those are the most common and persistent myths and misperceptions regarding the proper use of the language. Next, we'll turn our attention to the most frequently asked writing questions from writers and non-writers alike.

CHAPTER 25

A Language Handbook

Style Guide

Though I'd been taught at our dining room table about the solar system and knew the earth revolved around the sun, and our moon around us, I never found out the moon didn't come up in the west until I was a writer and Herschel Brickell, the literary critic, told me after I misplaced it in a story. He said valuable words to me about my new profession: Always be sure you get your moon in the right part of the sky.

—Eudora Welty

This chapter includes a potpourri of questions I've most commonly been asked over my several decades of teaching writing. It presents a miscellany of accepted styles for many common mechanics in writing, those that are a matter of preference as well as some that are a matter of right and wrong. You may have reason to choose a different style than that suggested here when the matter is one of preference. The important thing is to *have* a style and to be consistent in that convention. Consistency suggests an informed and deliberate approach and avoids the appearance of ignorance or carelessness. Having a style also keeps you from having to make and remake many small decisions when you're hassled or on deadline.

ages—Use numerals.

a.m., p.m.—Lower case.

an Hispanic—Avoid. Use *a Hispanic.*

an historic—Avoid. Use *a historic.*

anniversary—*Anno* and *annus* mean *year,* so "one-year anniversary" or "25-year anniversary" is redundant. Make it "first anniversary" or "25th anniversary." Structures such as "three-week anniversary" or "one-month anniversary" are incorrect.

apostrophes—P's and Q's. POWs (plural, not possessive). '90s.

autopsy—Avoid the redundant "autopsy to determine the cause of death."

backward—Not "backwards."

barbecue—No Q.

better, best—It's the *better* of the two, and the *best* of three or more.

capitalization—Avoid unnecessary capitals.

Capitalize proper but not common nouns. It's *President Doe,* but *the president; Pope John Paul II,* but *the pope;* the *Mississippi River,* but *the river.*

Capitalize job titles *before* names only if the titles are formal (unique to that job). For example, company chairman Don Doe or executive editor and senior vice president John Doe, but U.S. Trade Representative Sally Doe, Democratic Party Chairman Jane Doe, Prime Minister Jimmy Doe. There's no need to capitalize job titles that *follow* the person's name. (Capitalize any proper nouns in the title in all cases.)

Capitalize *department* only when it is part of a proper noun: Department of State, State Department.

Uppercase *city council* in relation to any specific council, but lowercase *council member.*

Some regions are uppercase: Gulf Coast (but "the gulf"); Northern Michigan and the Upper Peninsula; Northern and Southern California; South Florida, but northern Florida and upstate New York. East, west, north, and south are not capitalized when they refer to direction—that is, to compass points. (See also "Titles" below. Consult a dictionary for particular words and phrases.)

chaise longue—Not chaise "lounge."

citizens—Countries have *citizens*. Cities and states have *residents*. Monarchies have *subjects*.

colon—Avoid after a *be* verb: *No*: The three objectives of the new plan are: *Yes*: The new plan has three objectives: These are the three objectives of the new plan: Below are the new plan's three objectives:

commas—Below are common comma confusions.

- Avoid automatically placing commas between adjectives preceding a noun:
  No: His only memory was of a yellow, frame house.
  No: He was a charming, young reprobate.

Commas should not follow *yellow* or *charming*. *Yellow* modifies *frame house*—not just *house*; *charming* modifies *young reprobate*. If you're unsure, try the conjunction *and* where the comma would go: yellow *and* frame house, charming *and* young reprobate. If the resulting structure is odd, don't use a comma; that awkwardness shows that the adjectives are not separate and equal modifiers. *Yes*: the turreted red brick tower. *Yes*: an angry, ugly dog. (See also the quiz in Chapter 23, item and answer no. 7.)

- It is never wrong to include a comma before *and* in a series. Such has been the accepted practice in English for centuries, and many still prefer it. It is usually acceptable, however, to omit the serial comma if no confusion arises. But editors should refrain from automatically deleting it. It is not wrong, and the writer's preference should rule. (See a fuller discussion in Chapter 24 under the heading "Restoring the serial comma.")

• Don't place a comma after *and* or *but* at the beginning of a sentence unless if you are punctuating something else in the sentence:

No: And, it was a cold day.

Yes: And it was a cold day.

Yes: And, when he had finished the project, he resigned.

No: But, he resigned.

Yes: But he resigned.

Yes: But, hoping to avert a crisis, he resigned.

• Place commas at beginning *and* end of buried attribution.

No: After the confrontation, he said the president was angry.

Yes: After the confrontation, he said, the president was angry.

No: During the meeting, he said the board tried to humiliate him.

Yes: During the meeting, he said, the board tried to humiliate him.

The first incorrect example says he *made his statement* after the confrontation, when in fact he said that the *president was angry* after the confrontation. The second example says he *made his statement* during the meeting, when in fact he said the board *tried to humiliate him* during the meeting.

• Standard English usually sets off *too* from the rest of the sentence with commas: "He said that he, too, was going." If the sentence is brief and simple, however, and the *too* is at sentence's end, it often is acceptable to omit the comma: "I am going too."

• Place a comma before a conjunction midsentence if what follows the conjunction could stand as a complete sentence. Omit the comma if what follows is a fragment:

Yes: She is going, but she doesn't want to.

Yes: She is going but doesn't want to.

• The two most frequently missed commas occur when city and state appear midsentence, or when month, day, and year appear midsentence. Place a comma both *before* and *after* the state or the year:

Yes: He went to Los Angeles, Calif., on March 30, 2003, after receiving a summons from the chief. (Notice the commas *before* and *after* "Calif." and "2003.")

But: She has been in Denver, Colo., since *June 1995*. (No comma necessary between month and year when the day is absent.) But: He was in *Washington D.C.*, before that. (No comma after the city in this case; "D.C." is not a state.)

dove—The past tense of *dive* is *dived*.

eponym—See "namesake."

espresso—Not "expresso."

et. al., e.g., i.e.—*Et. al.* means "and others"; *e.g.* means "for example"; *i.e.* means "that is." Each should be lower case and italicized. Since Latin abbreviations call for special and possibly obtrusive treatment, it may be best to stick to the English *and others, for example, that is.*

etc.—Use commas both before *and* after *etc.* when it appears midsentence.

everyday (adjective), **every**

day (adverb)—everyday tasks; he wears it every day.

every time

female—Avoid as a noun when referring to a woman or women. Use as a noun only in specialized writing—for example, in medicine, statistics, police reports, sociology—or when referring to animals. Acceptable as an adjective in both common and technical use.

No: The author is a female.

Yes: The author is a woman.

free rein—Not "free reign." The expression refers to giving a horse his head.

hang on to, hold on to—Not *onto*.

historic, historical—*Historic* means important in history; *historical* means concerned with or about history.

hoi polloi—Greek expression that means *the many* and refers to the masses. Avoid with *the* (redundant), or to mean elite or upper class.

holdup (noun), **hold up** (verb)

housewife—Most stylebooks prefer *homemaker*.

irregardless—A double negative. Use *regardless*.

kindergartner—Not "kindergardner."

lady—Most stylebooks prefer *woman* except in formal titles (Lady Diana) or when the reference is to fine manners—and the latter only when appropriate and without patronizing overtones.

likely—Avoid as a substitute for *probably*. Not all words ending with *-ly* are adverbs, and *likely* is not. It's an adjective, parallel to the adjective *probable* rather than to the adverb *probably*. Therefore, *likely* behaves like an adjective, with a "be" verb usually preceding: *The situation is likely to worsen.* (Not: *The situation likely will worsen.*)

No: They likely will go.

Yes: They are likely to go.

Yes: They probably will go.

literally—It means *actually* and is the opposite of "figuratively." Avoid when speaking metaphorically. If you say the band *literally* exploded, it means the band *actually* exploded.

makeup (noun), **make up** (verb), **make-up** (adjective)

media—The plural of *medium*. Media *are*.

mid—Generally no hyphen unless it precedes a capital letter or numeral.

mini—Generally no hyphen: miniseries, miniskirt, minibus

minuscule—Not "miniscule."

Moslem—Most stylebooks prefer *Muslim*.

namesake, eponym—A *namesake* is a person or thing named after someone of something. The person or thing that provides the name is an *eponym*: German engineer Rudolf Diesel was the *eponym* for the diesel engine.

near miss—An illogical construction. Some object that a near miss would necessarily be a direct hit.

non—Generally not hyphenated (nonprofit, nonsmearing) except before a proper noun or in awkward constructions (nonnuclear).

numerals—The basic guideline: Write out the numerals one to nine; two digits or more: use numerals: *nine days ago; 10 days ago.* Avoid numerals at sentence beginnings.

one of the only—An illiteracy. Make it "one of the few," or some such.

online

onstage, offstage

orient (verb), **orientation** (noun)—Avoid "orientate." The proper noun, the Orient, is a geographical area.

parentheses—Punctuation goes *after* parentheses, not before, when the parenthesis appears within a sentence:

Would you prefer to have the banquet Sunday (if everyone else approves)?

I'd prefer Sunday (if everyone else approves).

After they nominated Jim (instead of *me!*), they called for a vote of acclamation.

She didn't want the job (or so she said), and no one pressed her on the issue.

percent; *%*—Use *percent* in text; the symbol *%* is for charts, graphs, tabulated material, lists, and the like.

police officer—Most stylebooks avoid *policeman, policewoman,* and *cop.*

postal service state abbreviations—At the moment, use traditional state abbreviations in text; reserve postal abbreviations for that purpose, or for lists, charts, or graphic material. This usage is probably in transition, but can confuse. For example, readers can confuse AR for Arkansas or Arizona; MA for Maine, Massachusetts, or Maryland; and MI for Michigan or Minnesota.

quotations: ellipses, brackets—For ellipses marking midsentence deletions in quotations, three spaced dots. Don't mark deletions at sentence beginning; just start the quotation there. An ellipsis at sentence end is four spaced dots, the last being the period.

Brackets identify editorial insertions. The practice is obtrusive and should be used only when necessary. Avoid multiple brackets in a quote—if the quote is so unclear that an editor has to explain it repeatedly, it should be paraphrased or made a partial quote. If you delete words before a bracketed insertion, the deletion should be marked with an ellipsis. This, too, is busy and obtrusive. It's better to paraphrase fuzzy quotes than to make them busy and unreadable.

quotations: periods and commas—Periods and commas always go *inside* quotation marks in American English.

reason is *because*, reason *why*—Redundant. Avoid such constructions as "the *reason* they canceled the meeting is *because* so few members showed up." Write instead "they canceled the meeting because" or "the reason they cancelled the meeting is that . . . ." *Reason why* also is redundant. "The reason *why* she works is to pay her tuition" should be "She works to pay her tuition," or "The reason she works is to pay her tuition."

re-creation—Hyphenate when meaning to create again rather than fun or leisure activity.

round trip (noun), **round-trip** (adjective)

Scot, Scots, Scottish—The correct terms for natives of Scotland. Avoid *Scotch*.

semi-colons—Can be used to separate two related but independent clauses, or in a list if there are commas in one or more of the other items in the list.

ship names—Capitalize. Refer to a ship with the pronoun *it* rather than with a feminine pronoun.

sic.—Latin for *thus* or *so*. Identifies an error in quoted material. Avoid. It's better to paraphrase.

single most, single best, single biggest, etc.—*Single* can't modify those superlatives. Put the word in front of what it *does* modify (most important single moment, best single day, biggest single donation). *Single* could be unnecessary in these constructions, in any case.

spit and image—Not "spittin'" or "spitting" image.

temblor—The earthquake term. Not "trembler."

the past decade, the past 10 years, etc.—Use the *last* decade, the *last* 10 years, etc. Of course that time is *past*.

these points forward; *those* points back: *These are the new officers; those were the officers last year.*

this points forward; *that* points back: *This is what he will do; that is what he did.*

times—Preferred usage is *from 7 to 9 p.m.* (not "from 7-9 p.m.") or *between 7 and 9 p.m.* (not "between 7-9 p.m.").

titles—Below are generally preferred styles for titles of various media.

• Reference works are capitalized but need neither italics nor quotation marks.

    Webster's New Collegiate
    Dictionary
    Texas Almanac
    The Dimwit's Dictionary
    Webster's New World Thesaurus

• Major sacred texts are capitalized but usually need neither italics nor quotation marks:

    Holy Bible; Bible
    Book of Common Prayer
    Book of Mormon
    second chapter of the Koran

• Books and other media: Italicize the titles and subtitles of published books, pamphlets, proceedings and collections, periodicals, and newspapers and sections of newspapers published separately *(New York Times Book Review)*.

• Italicize the titles of motion pictures, plays, and *continuing* series on television and radio. (But use quotation marks for *episodes* in a continuing series. See below.)

• Use quotation marks for the titles of short stories; short poems (italicize very long or book-length poems); essays; songs; lectures and speeches; studies and reports; unpublished works (such as dissertations); and course names. (Use quotation marks only with descriptive course titles, not with simple course labels denoting a major study area: English 101, biology, physics, beginning Spanish, conversational French, etc.) Examples:

He read *The Waste Land,* "The Lovesong of J. Alfred Prufrock," and "Kubla Khan" in a college course, "Poetry for the Novice."

During Professor Tweedle's favorite lecture, "The Archetype of the Mask in Claude Levi-Strauss' book, *The Raw and the Cooked,*" the raucous Texas audience suddenly began singing "Oklahoma!"

• Use quotation marks for *parts of works* such as chapters; articles in an anthology, encyclopedia, newspaper, or magazine; symphony movements; episodes in a continuing series, etc.:

The reader was referring to an article in *The Dallas Morning News* headlined "Elderly man kills wife, himself."

Next week's offering on *Mystery!* will be "Colonel Mustard in the Library With a Knife."

When a *continuing* series presents a *limited* series, both series titles are italicized, and the individual episodes stand in quotation marks:

Masterpiece Theatre will present the episode "Casualties" tonight on its *Fortunes of War* series.

• Popular music: Italicize album titles, but use quotation marks for *song* titles:

• "One Way Ticket," a single from *Blue,* was a hit more than a decade ago.

• Classical music: Italicize titles of operas, oratorios, motets, tone poems, and program- oriented works (that is, works that tell a story): *Carmen* Vivaldi's *Four Seasons*

• Use quotation marks for songs from operas and symphonies that are part of larger works:

"Spring" from *The Four Seasons*

• Use neither quotation marks nor italics for titles of works that are merely musical *forms* (symphonies, sonatas, concertos):

Beethoven's Symphony No. 6

Adagio from the Fifth Symphony

- Italicize descriptive or alternate titles of longer works.
  William Tell Overture
  Beethoven's *Emperor* Concerto
  Beethoven's Symphony No. 6 is also known as *The Pastorale*.
- Paintings and sculpture: Italicize official titles of paintings, drawings, statues, and other works of art. Traditional but unofficial names usually stand in capitalized roman, no quotes:
  The Thinker by Rodin; Rodin's *Thinker*
  Hogarth's series of drawings *The Rake's Progress*
  The official name of Leonardo's Mona Lisa is *La Gioconda*.
- Software and CD-ROM products: Operating systems and programs, tools, games, and reference works are capitalized, no quotes: DOS, Quicken, Eudora, Monopoly, Encarta.
- Capitalize the first and last words of a title and all the principal words between (nouns, pronouns, adjectives, verbs, adverbs, and subordinate conjunctions such as *if, because, as, that*, etc.). Lowercase articles *(a, an, the)*; *to* (both as preposition and in infinitives); coordinating conjunctions *(for, and, nor, but, or, yet, so)*; and prepositions of fewer than four letters. Capitalize prepositions of four or more letters. (Style guides differ, but this treatment follows the major stylebooks. Longer prepositions such as *between, toward, beyond, among, with, from*, and so forth often look odd if not wrong when they're lowercased in titles.)
  "What Kind of Fool Am I?"
  "What to Listen For"
  "Stopping by Woods on a Snowy Evening"
  "Hand in Hand With a Man Called Dan"
  "Thirteen Ways of Looking at a Blackbird"
- A title is a singular noun and takes a singular verb: *Brief Lives* is considered a biographical companion to the arts.
- The initial article *A, An,* or *The* in titles may prove awkward in text and should be omitted if:
  The article follows a possessive noun or pronoun.
  No: Hoffer's philosophy was well presented in his *The True Believer*.

Yes: Hoffer's philosophy was well presented in his *True Believer*.

The article follows an adjective or another article:

No: She cited a The Oxford Universal Dictionary definition.

Yes: She cited an Oxford Universal Dictionary definition.

• A title should not be used as the object of a preposition such as *on* or *about*—as in, for example, the designation of a topic:

No: In his well-known book on *Modern English Usage*, Fowler discusses the use of italics for emphasis.

Yes: In his well-known book, *Modern English Usage*, Fowler . . . .

Yes: In his well-known book on English usage, Fowler . . . .

toward—Not "towards."

verbal agreement—Avoid using for *oral* agreement. The preferred meaning of *verbal* is words, written *and* spoken. A verbal agreement therefore can mean *either* a written or an oral contract. Use *oral* or *spoken* agreement if the agreement is not in writing.

wait—Wait *for,* not *on* (unless the reference is to waiting on tables).

zero—Cut meaningless numerals:

7:00 p.m. = 7 p.m. But 7:30 p.m.

$1 million; $1.6 billion

Credits, Permissions, and Acknowledgments

Grateful acknowledgment is made for permission to use the following:

Chapter 1

Excerpt from *The Right Stuff* by Tom Wolfe. Copyright © 1979 by Tom Wolfe. Reprinted by permission of Farrar, Straus and Giroux, LLC.

Excerpt from *The Night Manager* by John le Carré. Reprinted by permission of Ballantine.

Chapter 15

Random House, Inc. and Sterling Lord Literistic (Canada and UK) for *Simisola* by Ruth Rendell.

From A Traitor to Memory by Elizabeth George, copyright © 2001 by Susan Elizabeth George. Used by permission of Bantam Books, a division of Random House, Inc.

Reprinted with the permission of Scribner, an imprint of Simon and Schuster Adult Publishing Group, from *Writing for Story* by Jon Franklin. Copyright © 1986 by Jon Franklin.

Chapter 14

The Dallas Morning News for David Casstevens article.

Chapter 16

Random House, Inc. for *Shake Hands Forever* by Ruth Rendell.

Two very brief quotations from pp. 169, 228 from *Bandits* by Elmore Leonard. Copyright © 1987 by Elmore Leonard. Reprinted by permission of HarperCollins Publishers Inc.

Excerpt from pp. 54-6 from *Cuba Libre* by Elmore Leonard. Copyright © 1998 by Elmore Leonard. Reprinted by permission of HarperCollins Publishers Inc.

Chapter 17

Excerpt from *Coming Into the* Country by John McPhee. Copyright © 1977 by John McPhee. Reprinted by permission of Farrar, Straus and Giroux, LLC.

Excerpt from *The Night Manager* by John le Carré. Reprinted by permission of Ballantine.

Reprinted with the permission of Scribner, an imprint of Simon and Schuster Adult Publishing Group, from *Innocent Blood* by P.D. James. Copyright © 1980 by P.D. James.

Random House, Inc. for *A Certain Justice* by P.D. James.

Random House, Inc. for *A Taste for Death* by P.D. James.

The Dallas Morning News for Russell Smith and David Casstevens excerpts.

Chapter 18

Random House, Inc. for *Devices and Desires* by P.D. James.

Random House, Inc. for *Deception on His Mind* by Elizabeth George.

Random House, Inc. for *Atonement* by Ian McEwan.

Reprinted with the permission of Simon and Schuster Adult Publishing Group, from *Catch-22* by Joseph Heller. Copyright renewed © 1989 by Joseph Heller.

Random House, Inc. for *Missing Joseph* by Elizabeth George.

The Dallas Morning News for Rick Holter excerpt.

Chapter 19

Little, Brown and Company for *Le Convict and Other Stories* by James Lee Burke.

Excerpt from *A Small Town in Germany* by John le Carré. Reprinted by permission of Pocket Books.

The Dallas Morning News for excerpts from Brad Bailey, Jeremy Gerard, and Christine Wicker.

Chapter 20

Reprinted with the permission of Scribner, an imprint of Simon and Schuster Adult Publishing Group, from *On Writing: A Memoir of the Craft* by Stephen King. Copyright © 2000 by Stephen King.

Made in the USA
Columbia, SC
14 January 2021